THE BOOK OF
Chilies & Stews

THE BOOK OF
Chilies & Stews

Sara Davis

HPBooks

HPBooks
A member of Penguin Group (USA) Inc.
375 Hudson Street, New York, New York 10014, USA
Penguin Group (Canada), 10 Alcorn Avenue, Toronto,
Ontario M4V 3B2, Canada (a division of Pearson Penguin
Canada Inc.)
Penguin Books Ltd., 80 Strand, London WC2R 0RL, England
Penguin Group Ireland, 25 St. Stephen's Green, Dublin 2,
Ireland (a division of Penguin Books Ltd.)
Penguin Group (Australia), 250 Camberwell Road,
Camberwell, Victoria 3124, Australia (a division of Pearson
Australia Group Pty. Ltd.)
Penguin Books India Pvt. Ltd., 11 Community Centre,
Panchsheel Park, New Delhi—110 017, India
Penguin Group (NZ), cnr. Airborne and Rosedale Roads,
Albany, Auckland 1310, New Zealand (a division of Pearson
New Zealand Ltd.)
Penguin Books (South Africa) (Pty.) Ltd., 24 Sturdee Avenue,
Rosebank, Johannesburg 2196, South Africa
Penguin Books Ltd., Registered Offices: 80 Strand, London
WC2R 0RL, England

Copyright © 2005 by Salamander Books,
By arrangement with Salamander Books

An imprint of Chrysalis Books Group plc

Photographer: Philip Wilkins
Home Economist and Stylist: Mandy Phipps
Editor: Lesley Wilson
Designer: Cara Hamilton
Production: Kate Rogers
Filmset and reproduction by: Anorax Imaging Ltd

All rights reserved. No part of this book may be reproduced,
scanned, or distributed in any printed or electronic form
without permission. Please do not participate in or encourage
piracy of copyrighted materials in violation of the author's
rights. Purchase only authorized editions.

ISBN: 1-55788-474-9

PRINTING HISTORY
HPBooks trade paperback edition / October 2005

Notice: The information contained in this book is true and
complete to the best of our knowledge. All recommendations
are made without any guarantees on the part of the author or
the publisher. The author and publisher disclaim all liability in
connection with the use of this information.

Printed and bound in China

10 9 8 7 6 5 4 3 2 1

CONTENTS

INTRODUCTION 6

VEGETARIAN 12

BEEF 28

PORK & LAMB 46

POULTRY & GAME 65

FISH & SEAFOOD 84

INDEX 96

INTRODUCTION

Stews and chilies are the ultimate comfort food and have a wide appeal. As well as being easy dishes to cook, they're also economical because the cheaper, less popular cuts of meat are perfect for long, slow cooking which makes them tender and succulent.

What is a stew? It is a combination of ingredients, which could be meat and vegetables, or even just vegetables, cooked on top of the stove in a liquid. A stew has less liquid than a soup, but more liquid than a casserole and is simmered for a long period.

Cooking ingredients in liquid, especially meat, keeps it moist and helps to break down tough connective tissue. The liquid itself can be almost anything from ordinary meat, vegetable, or fish stock to beer, wine, or simply water.

Prepare stews the day before you need them, if you have time or if it is more convenient, then simply reheat the following day. The flavor of the stew will improve overnight.

What is a chili? There are conflicting definitions of what constitutes a chili—if you ask a Texan, they will tell you to use chopped beef, lots of hot chilies and absolutely no beans. Texans love to hold chili cook-offs, in which beans are absolutely forbidden by the rules.

Outside of Texas, however, people will probably think of the dish chili con carne—literally translated from Spanish as "chili with meat" which usually has red kidney beans and a traditional mix of spices, including cumin, paprika, and hot chilies. Other recipes use a mixture of vegetables, such as onions, carrots, and celery, to add flavor. However, what you put in your chili is up to you!

WHAT GOES INTO THE POT?

Beef: Beef has a rich flavor and many cuts are suited to slow-cooking. Choose cuts from the moving parts of the animal as these have more connective tissue, which breaks down during slow cooking to produce a rich gravy or sauce.

Pork: The same rules apply when choosing cuts of pork for slow cooking. Although trotters have very little meat on them, adding one to a slow cooked stew will add an unbelievable richness to the finished dish. You can also choose to stew rib cuts which, when slow cooked, will become meltingly tender.

Lamb: Choosing lamb is slightly different as the animals tend to be much younger, and therefore more tender. Cuts for stewing are best from the neck, fore shank, and breast as well as the shoulder. Lamb also requires much less cooking time (about a third less) to make even the toughest cuts succulent.

Poultry and Game: Chicken lends itself to stewing because slow cooking in liquid leaves chicken meat very tender and falling from the bones, but use legs and in particular thighs if the cooking time is going to be lengthy as breast meat will dry out, even if cooked in liquid, after about 45 minutes cooking.

Game birds are excellent for braising, as they tend to be lean so cooking in liquid helps keep them moist. The addition of a fatty meat, such as bacon, adds flavor as well as moisture. Be careful when cooking duck as, unlike other game birds, it is very fatty and this will need to be trimmed away before cooking or skimmed off before serving.

Venison makes great stew, but is also a lean meat so keep an eye on it to prevent it overcooking and drying out. Choose shoulder or leg meat and check it before the end of the cooking time to make sure that it hasn't dried out.

Seafood: Seafood stews are the quickest of all, because most seafood requires very little cooking. As a general rule, the sauce is cooked first and the seafood added at the end until just cooked through—often a matter of minutes. The sauce might be a rustic stew of tomatoes, white wine, and garlic or a more sophisticated sauce of saffron and cream. Any kind of seafood is suitable, but in particular shellfish and meatier fish, such as red snapper and angler fish, are excellent for making stews.

Vegetables: Vegetables play an important role in slow-cooked dishes. They add flavor but they can also add texture and body to the finished dish. Root vegetables in particular are excellent, as they hold their shape well and have distinctive flavors. Other vegetables, such as peas or green beans, corn, and broccoli, can be added toward the end of cooking to add color and freshness. Potatoes are great in stews because they add bulk and texture and can act as a thickener, but be careful not to add them too early because they will break down.

A NOTE ON CHILIES

Fresh chilies are a very important ingredient when making chili of all kinds. A bewildering variety of fresh and dried chilies are now available in grocery and specialist stores as well as online and by mail order.

Chilies can be rated for heat on the Scoville Scale (after Wilbur Scoville, 1912 who developed a rating scale). The scale measures the amount of capsaicin in the pepper in Scoville units—the greater the number of Scoville units, the hotter the chili!

In fresh chilies, the capsaicin is concentrated in the membranes and seeds, so these should be removed if you want to reduce the heat. In dried chilies, the capsaicin is concentrated in the dried flesh so removing the seeds won't reduce the heat.

USING SPICES

Spices are integral to the preparation of a good chili—and a number of stews as well. Ground spices have a relatively short shelf life, so keep an eye on the expiration date and discard in any case after six months. Spices are brought to life by frying, which releases their essential oils. Always add spices to the hot pan before adding any liquid, and allow them to cook for a minute or so.

Turmeric: It has a slightly bitter but very pungent flavor, is very popular in East Indian cooking, and is almost

Below: *From the top center, clockwise: birds eye, scotch bonnet, dried green jalepeño, large green peppers/capsicum, mixed red and green "seranade," mixed finger chillies, crushed red chillies, and dried red whole chillies.*

always used in curry preparations. Ground turmeric is widely available in stores but you will have to go to specialist stores to find it fresh. Use in stews with an Eastern influence.

Coriander: It's known for both its seeds (actually the dried, ripe fruit of the plant) and for its dark green, lacy leaves (also called cilantro). The flavors of the seeds and leaves bear absolutely no resemblance to each other. The tiny, yellow-tan seeds are mildly fragrant and have an aromatic flavor akin to a combination of lemon, sage, and caraway. Coriander adds a warm, slightly sweet note to a chili or curry.

Cumin: The seeds look similar to caraway seeds but have a warmer, earthier flavor, and aroma. Also available ground, cumin is most commonly used in Mediterranean, Asian, and Middle Eastern dishes and is a constituent of chili powder. Dry roasting the seeds intensifies their flavor and, in this way, make an excellent garnish for chilies and stews.

Nutmeg: Egg-shaped and about 1-inch long, nutmeg has a warm, spicy, and sweet aroma and is often used as a seasoning, much like black pepper, to complement other flavors. Use it freshly ground rather than ready ground, as its delicate fragrance is short-lived. Nutmeg is often used in conjunction with other spices in chilies, but will be useful in stews containing vegetables, particularly spinach.

Mace: Similar in flavor to nutmeg but deeper and more pungent mace is the dried bright yellowish-red membrane that surrounds the nutmeg seed. Sold whole (as "blade" mace) and ground, it is used in both sweet and savory dishes. Mace is particularly popular in very traditional dishes.

Cloves: Dark reddish-brown and shaped liked small nails, they have a very warm and pungent flavor. Cloves are available whole or ground and should be used sparingly. You will find cloves used in chilies and stews with a North African or West Indian influence.

Chili Powder: Not to be confused with ground chili or cayenne, chili powder is a mixture of dried chilies, garlic, oregano, cumin, coriander, cloves, and sometimes salt. However, the mixture can vary enormously from brand to brand, so check the label carefully. Chili powder is usually available in mild, medium, or hot.

Below: *From middle top, clockwise: szechuan pepper, cumin, mace and saffron strands, turmeric, chili powder and cinnamon, and coriander.*

CHILIES & STEWS

Cinnamon: Cinnamon is either sold as cinnamon sticks or ground to make cinnamon powder. Although generally used in sweet dishes, it makes an interesting addition to savory stews and curries.

Saffron: A little goes a long way. Saffron adds an aromatic, almost buttery, flavor to a number of classic stews, such as bouillabase, and rice dishes, such as paella and risotto Milanese. Always buy saffron whole and grind it yourself, as the powdered varieties lose their appeal quickly.

Szechuan Pepper: Szechuan pepper has a distinctive warm flavor and fragrance and is useful in Asian stews. It can be found in stores, Asian markets, and specialty stores in whole or ground form.

Cardamom: Papery, light green cardamom pods each contain a number of tiny seeds. Put the pods into a mortar and pound lightly with a pestle to release the seeds then crush the seeds before using. Cardamom has a pungent aroma and a distinctive warm spicy flavor. It is commonly used in savory dishes, especially in East Indian cooking. It is best purchased in pods and treated as above, rather than ready ground. A little goes a long way.

Paprika: Its flavor can range from mild and sweet to pungent and hot and the color can be anything from bright orange red to a deep blood red. Most paprika comes from Spain, South America, California, or Hungary, with Hungarian varieties considered superior. It is also available smoked. Paprika adds a sweet and/or hot red pepper flavor to chilies and stews.

Cayenne: A hot, pungent powder made from a mixture of varieties of dried hot red chilies. It is used mainly to add chili heat to a dish.

USING HERBS

Fresh herbs are readily available nowadays. You can substitute dried, of course (use about third of the amount given in the recipe) but the flavor will not be the same. Fresh herbs add a vibrant flavor to food that is irreplaceable. In general, the more woody herbs like rosemary and thyme will be added at the beginning of cooking time in order to add a subtle flavor throughout the dish. More tender herbs, like cilantro and basil, are usually chopped and added at the end of cooking or even after cooking as a garnish as their flavor will be impaired by the heat if they are cooked too long.

Thyme: A member of the mint family, thyme is a perennial herb native to southern Europe and the Mediterranean. Fresh thyme adds a fresh, almost lemony flavor and aroma and has an affinity with almost all meats. It is excellent in stews and can be added as whole sprigs, or the leaves can be stripped from the stalks first. Add it at the beginning of the cooking time.

Parsley: This slightly peppery, fresh-flavored herb is commonly used as a flavoring and garnish. Though there are more than 30 varieties of this herb, the most popular are curly-leaf parsley and the more strongly flavored Italian or flat-leaf parsley. Generally, add chopped parsley just before serving, as cooking can destroy its flavor. Alternatively, choose pretty sprigs to garnish.

Rosemary: Rosemary's silver-green, needle-shaped leaves are highly aromatic and their flavor has hints of both lemon and pine. As with thyme, add whole sprigs of rosemary at the beginning of cooking, or strip the leaves from the stalks and chop finely. Rosemary has a particular affinity with lamb, but also goes well with chicken and fish.

Oregano: This herb, sometimes called wild marjoram, belongs to the mint family and is related to both marjoram and thyme. Oregano has a strong, pungent flavor and aroma. Because of its pungency, it requires a bit of caution in its use. Mediterranean oregano is milder than the Mexican variety, which is generally used in highly spiced dishes, such as chilies. Oregano is one of the few herbs which is preferable dried in some dishes, as drying seems to temper its pungency. It is best used in tomato-based stews and chilies.

THE BOOK OF

Above: *From top left, clockwise: sage, chives, basil, lemon thyme, parsley, rosemary, cilantro*

Sage: The narrow, oval, gray-green leaves of this pungent herb are slightly bitter and have a musty mint taste and aroma. Add to stews at the beginning of cooking or add sparingly toward the end. Sage is also excellent dried, but use about one third of the specified fresh quantity.

Cilantro: Cilantro the bright green leaves and stems of the coriander plant. Cilantro has a lively, pungent fragrance that some describe as "soapy." It is widely used in Asian, Caribbean, and Latin American cooking and its distinctive flavor lends itself to highly spiced foods, especially chilies.

Basil: Fresh basil has a pungent flavor that can be described as a cross between licorice and cloves. It's a key herb in Mediterranean cooking, essential to the delicious Italian pesto, and is excellent in tomato-based stews.

Chives: Related to the onion and leek, this fragrant herb has slender, vivid green, hollow stems. Chives have a mild onion flavor and should be used toward the end of cooking in order to preserve the fresh flavor. Use as a garnish, snipped over a stew.

Tarragon: Tarragon has narrow, pointed, dark green leaves and a distinctive anise-like flavor. Tarragon has a particular affinity with chicken and is excellent in creamy dishes. Use sparingly, however, as its flavor can easily dominate.

CHILI'S LITTLE HELPERS

Tortillas:
Both flour and corn tortillas are readily available in stores, but homemade ones can't be beaten for freshness and flavor. Add toasted cumin seeds, or a few crushed dried chilies, to either recipe for a twist on the classic tortilla.

Flour Tortilla:
1 lb all-purpose or whole wheat flour
1 tablespoon salt

6 tablespoons lard or vegetable shortening
1 cup hot water

Sift flour and salt into a mixing bowl and rub in the lard or vegetable shortening, until mixture resembles fine bread crumbs. Mix in water gradually to form a soft, pliable dough. Whole wheat flour may need more water. Knead on a well-floured surface until smooth and no longer sticky. Cover with a damp dish towel.

Cut off about 3 tablespoons of dough at a time, keeping the rest covered. Knead into a ball. Roll the ball of dough out into a very thin circle with a floured rolling pin. If you like, cut into a neat circle using a 10-inch plate as a guide. Continue until all the dough is used.

Stack the tortillas as you make them—flouring each will help to prevent sticking. Cover with a clean dish towel. Heat a heavy-bottom skillet and carefully place in a tortilla. Cook for about 10 seconds per side until tinged with brown. Stack and keep covered until all are cooked. Use according to chosen recipe.

Corn Tortillas:
1½ cups masa harina
2 teaspoons salt
2 teaspoons lard or vegetable shortening
1¼ cups water

In a medium bowl, stir together the masa harina and salt. In a small pan over high heat, bring the lard or shortening and water to a boil and stir until melted.

Pour this liquid into the masa harina and blend well with a fork or pastry blender. Knead on a lightly floured board until smooth, about 5 minutes. Divide the dough into 12 pieces and roll each into a ball about 1-inch in diameter. Roll out the dough between pieces of parchment or waxed paper until the dough is paper thin and about 6 inches in diameter. Alternatively, press the pieces of dough in a tortilla press.

Heat a large cast-iron or other heavy skillet over high heat until very hot. Remove a circle of dough from the paper and place it in the hot skillet. Cook until brown on one side, about 30 seconds, turn and brown the other side. Keep warm in a dish towel. Repeat until all the tortillas are made.

Tostadas:
Make the flour or corn tortilla dough as above, but divide the dough into smaller pieces to make circles about 6 inches in diameter.

Heat about 1 inch of oil in a large skillet to 375F (190C), or until a cube of bread browns in 60 seconds. Carefully lower tortillas, one at a time, into the hot oil until completely submerged. Deep-fry until golden, crisp, and puffed up.

Drain on paper towels and serve as soon as possible, topped with refried beans, shredded chicken or beef, salsa, cheese, etc. Great as an appetizer.

Taco Shells:
It is fairly easy to make taco shells at home, but to make your tacos a little special, you can make interesting shapes that you can then fill—and the flavor surpasses that of any commercial shell.

Make corn tortillas as above. Fill a deep pan or deep-fat fryer one third full with vegetable oil. Heat to 375F (190C), or until a cube of bread browns in 60 seconds.

Using two sets of tongs, grab a tortilla on opposite sides and lift it so it's shaped roughly like a taco shell. Carefully lower the tortilla into the oil, allowing the bottom, curved bit to set a little before lowering whole the whole tortilla into the oil. Cook for about 45 seconds–1 minute until crisp and lightly golden.

Drain on paper towels and repeat with remaining tortillas. You can also try using a ladle and lowering a tortilla into the oil, then press down using the back of a ladle to make a large basket-shape. Drain on paper towels as before.

Tortilla Chips:
Cut either flour or corn tortillas into 8 wedges each; set aside. Pour oil into a heavy pan or skillet to a depth of 1 inch.

Heat to a temperature of 375F (190C), or until a tortilla chip browns in 60 seconds. Drop the tortilla wedges into the hot oil in batches and cook for 1–2 minutes, or until they turn golden.

Drain the chips on paper towels and sprinkle with salt while still hot. Let cool and serve immediately or store in airtight containers.

THE BOOK OF

BLACK BEAN TACOS

2 tablespoons olive oil
1 onion, finely chopped
4 garlic cloves, finely chopped
2 fresh green chilies, seeded and chopped
2 teaspoons ground cumin
1 tablespoon dried oregano
1 lb cooked black beans (1¹/₃ cups dry weight)
²/₃ cup frozen corn kernels
1 (14-oz) can chopped tomatoes
1¹/₄ cups vegetable broth
salt and pepper, to taste
peanut oil, for frying
8 corn tortillas
1 recipe Roast Corn Chili Sauce (opposite), heated

Heat the oil in a pan and gently fry the onion and garlic for 5 minutes, until translucent. Add the chili, cumin, and oregano and stir-fry for 1 minute to release the flavor. Stir in the remaining ingredients, bring to a boil, and let simmer for 20 minutes, stirring occasionally, until most of the liquid has evaporated. Meanwhile, prepare the Roast Corn Chili Sauce as directed. Pan-fry the tortillas in 1 inch of oil over a medium high heat 30 seconds, until slightly browned. Drain on paper towels and keep warm while you fry the rest.

Form each tortilla into a boat shape in the palm of your hand, spoon in some of the filling and top with the heated sauce. They will become crisp as you do so. Transfer to a warm serving dish into which all the tacos will just fit and serve immediately.

Serves 4–8

CHILIES & STEWS

ROAST CORN CHILI SAUCE

2 ears corn with husks
2 fresh green chilies
2 tablespoons vegetable oil
1/2 onion, chopped
1 garlic clove, finely chopped
generous 1 cup vegetable broth
1 1/4 cups light cream
1 oz fresh cilantro, stalk removed
2 tablespoons lime juice
salt, to taste

Heat the oven to 350F (180C) and roast the corn in their husks for 10 minutes, turning occasionally. Add the chilies and roast for another 10 minutes.

Let cool then remove the husks and cut the kernels from the cobs. Cut each cob stalk into 3 pieces. Peel the chilies and remove the seeds. Heat the oil in a pan and gently fry the cob stalks, onion, and garlic for 3–4 minutes, until the onion is translucent. Add the broth, increase the heat, and let simmer for 10 minutes, until the liquid is reduced slightly. Add the cream and let simmer for 10 minutes, stirring continuously as the liquid reduces.

Remove the cob pieces with a slotted spoon, scraping off as much sauce as possible. Add to the sauce two-thirds of the corn kernels, the chilies, cilantro, and lime juice. Process in a blender until smooth. Stir in the remaining kernels. Season with salt, reheat, and serve.

Makes scant 2 1/2 cups

CHILI BEAN QUESADILLAS

1 (15-oz) can chili beans
4 large flour tortillas
3 scallions, chopped
2 ripe avocados, peeled and sliced
2 tomatoes, coarsely chopped
3 tablespoons chopped fresh cilantro
1 1/4 cups grated cheddar or Jack cheese
1 lime, juice only
1/2 cup sour cream

Preheat the broiler to medium. Put the beans into a bowl and mash coarsely with a potato masher, until thickened but some whole beans remain.

To assemble, put one tortilla onto a baking sheet or broiler pan and top with half the beans. Sprinkle over half the scallions, half the sliced avocado, half the tomatoes, half the cilantro, and finally, half the cheese. Squeeze over a little lime juice and half the sour cream in dollops. Top with a second tortilla and press down lightly.

Place under the broiler, until golden and crisp. Carefully turn the quesadilla over (the easiest way is to put a second baking sheet on top and invert together) and toast the second side. Remove from the heat and cut into wedges to serve. Repeat with the remaining ingredients.

Serves 4–6

CHILIES & STEWS

SWEET POTATO BURRITOS

2 tablespoons vegetable oil
1 medium sweet potato, cut into ½-inch dice
1 large onion, finely chopped
4 large garlic cloves, minced
1 fresh green chili, finely chopped
1 tablespoon ground cumin
1 tablespoon ground coriander
1 (15-oz) can black beans, drained and rinsed
3 tablespoons chopped fresh cilantro
2 tablespoons fresh lime juice
1 teaspoon salt
8 (8-inch) flour or corn tortillas
¾ cups grated cheese
fresh tomato salsa

Preheat the oven to 350F (180C). Heat the oil in a large skillet. Add the sweet potato, onion, garlic, and chili. Cook over medium heat for 10 minutes, adding a splash of water now and then, until the potato is tender and everything is lightly golden. Add the cumin and coriander and cook for 2–3 minutes longer, stirring. Remove from heat and set aside. In a large bowl, mix the sweet potato mixture, black beans, cilantro, lime juice, and salt. Mash coarsely using a potato masher, until the mixture starts to come together, but still has some texture.

Lightly oil a large baking dish. Put a generous spoonful of the filling in the center of each tortilla, roll it up, and place it, seam side down, in an oiled baking dish. Cover tightly with foil and bake for about 30 minutes, until piping hot. Remove the foil and sprinkle with the cheese. Return to the oven for 5 minutes or until the cheese has melted. Serve immediately, topped with salsa.

Serves 4

THE BOOK OF

TACO SAUCE

1 tablespoon olive oil
1 onion, chopped
1 green bell pepper, diced
$^1\!/_2$–1 red or green chili
$^1\!/_2$ teaspoon ground cumin
$^1\!/_2$ teaspoon ground coriander
$^1\!/_2$ garlic clove, minced
pinch of sugar, salt, and pepper
1 (14-oz) can chopped tomatoes
1 tablespoon tomato paste (optional)

Heat the oil in a heavy-bottom pan and, when hot, add the onion and bell pepper. Cook slowly to soften slightly. Chop the chili and add with the cumin, coriander, and garlic. Cook for another 2–3 minutes.

Add sugar, salt, pepper, and tomatoes with their juice. Cook another 5–6 minutes over medium heat to reduce and thicken slightly. Add tomato paste for color, if necessary. Taste and season again with salt and pepper, if desired, and use hot or cold according to your recipe.

Makes around 1 pint

CHILIES & STEWS

RED BEAN CHILI

1⅓ cups dried red kidney beans, soaked overnight
3 tablespoons oil
2 medium onions, chopped
1 bay leaf
1-inch piece cinnamon stick
6 cloves
seeds of 6 green cardamoms, ground
1½–2 green chilies, quartered
3 garlic cloves, minced
1-inch piece fresh ginger, peeled and grated
½ teaspoon chili powder
¼ teaspoon turmeric
1½ teaspoons ground coriander
1 teaspoon ground cumin
1 (14-oz) can chopped tomatoes
½ teaspoon salt

2–3 fresh cilantro sprigs, leaves chopped

Cook the kidney beans, boiling them rapidly for 10 minutes and then simmering for at least 30 minutes, until they are soft. Remove from the heat and let them cool in the cooking liquid. Heat the oil in a large pan and cook the onions, until they are soft. Add the bay leaf, cinnamon, cloves, and cardamoms and fry for 1 minute.

Add the green chilies, garlic, and ginger, and fry for about 30 seconds, before mixing in the ground spices and cooking for another 30 seconds, stirring continuously, to prevent them burning. Add the tomatoes and season with salt. Drain the beans and reserve the cooking liquid. Add the beans to the tomatoes and mix well, bring to a boil, then stir in 1¼ cups of the bean liquid. Let simmer for 10 minutes, then stir in the chopped cilantro.

Serves 4

─ SQUASH & BLACK BEAN CHILI ─

2 tablespoons vegetable oil
1 large onion, chopped
1 red bell pepper, seeded and coarsely chopped
1 green chili, seeded and finely chopped
2 garlic cloves, finely chopped
2 tablespoons chili powder
2 teaspoons ground cumin
1 teaspoon dried oregano
1 medium butternut squash, cut into 1-inch pieces
generous 1 cup vegetable broth
1 (14-oz) can chopped tomatoes
1 (15-oz) can black beans, drained and rinsed
scant 1 cup canned, fresh or frozen corn kernels
salt and freshly ground black pepper, to taste
chopped fresh cilantro, to serve
sour cream, to serve

Heat the oil in a large pan over medium heat. Add the onion, red bell pepper, and green chili and cook until softened, 5–8 minutes, stirring frequently. Add the garlic, chili powder, cumin, and oregano and cook for another minute, stirring constantly.

Add the squash, broth, tomatoes, and black beans, and stir to combine. Bring to a boil. Reduce the heat, cover, and let simmer for 30 minutes, stirring occasionally. Add the corn and cook for 5 minutes, or until tender, stirring occasionally. Season with salt and pepper and serve sprinkled with fresh cilantro and a spoonful of sour cream.

Serves 4

TOFU CHILI

2 tablespoons vegetable oil
1 lb 2 oz tofu, drained and cut into small cubes
1 red onion, finely chopped
2 garlic cloves, finely chopped
1 red bell pepper, seeded and chopped
1 green bell pepper, seeded and chopped
1 green chili, seeded and finely chopped
1 teaspoon ground cumin
1 tablespoon chili powder
1 teaspoon turmeric
3 tomatoes, peeled and coarsely chopped
1 (15-oz) can chili beans
2 teaspoons soy sauce
1 teaspoon lemon juice
2 tablespoons chopped fresh cilantro

Heat the oil over high heat in a large skillet or preheated wok. Fry the tofu cubes until golden and remove to a plate. Set aside. Add the onion, garlic, bell peppers, and chili to the pan and stir-fry until softened and starting to brown. Add the cumin, chili powder, and turmeric and stir well. Cook for another minute before adding the tomatoes and $1/2$ cup water. Add the beans and bring to a boil. Let simmer for 30 minutes uncovered, until thickened and the vegetables are tender.

Return the tofu to the pan and heat through. Add the soy sauce, lemon juice, and fresh cilantro. Serve hot.

Serves 4

BLACK & WHITE BEAN CHILI

CORNMEAL (POLENTA):
generous 1²/₃ cups cornmeal (polenta)
1¹/₄ teaspoons salt
4 cups water
olive oil, for oiling and brushing
CHILI:
1 teaspoon cumin seeds
2 teaspoons coriander seeds
2 teaspoons dried oregano
2 tablespoons olive oil
2 onions, chopped
2 garlic cloves, finely chopped
2 red bell peppers, seeded, and cut into ¹/₂-inch dice
¹/₄–1 teaspoon chili powder
2 (14-oz) cans chopped tomatoes
3 tablespoons tomato paste

1 teaspoon each of sugar and salt
2 cups canned black or kidney beans (about 18 oz)
1 cup canned navy beans (about 9 oz)
2¹/₂ cups vegetable broth
3 tablespoons chopped cilantro or flat-leaf parsley

Put cornmeal, salt, and water in a pan and stir. Slowly bring to a boil, stirring, then pour into an oiled 8 x 8-inch roasting dish. Cover with foil and bake at 400F (200C) for 1 hour. Cool slightly, turn out and leave to become firm. Toast the cumin and coriander in a dry skillet over medium heat. Add the oregano, toast for 10 seconds.

Lightly crush the mixture in a mortar. Heat the oil in a pan. Add the onions, garlic, bell peppers, spice mixture, and chili powder. Fry over medium heat for 5 minutes. Add the tomatoes, tomato paste, sugar, salt, beans, and broth. Stir and bring to a boil. Cover and simmer for 45 minutes. Add cilantro and simmer for 5 minutes. To make the crostini, cut the cornmeal into diamond-shapes, brush with olive oil, and toast under a preheated broiler.

Serves 6–8

CHILIES & STEWS

VEGETARIAN CHILI

2 medium onions, sliced
2 garlic cloves, chopped
1 tablespoon olive oil
2 tablespoons chili powder
1 tablespoon cumin
2 teaspoons paprika
1 (14-oz) can chopped tomatoes
generous 1 cup vegetable broth
1 large eggplant, cut into 1/2-inch cubes
2 green bell peppers, seeded, and cut into 1/2-inch dice
9 oz canned chickpeas, drained
9 oz canned red kidney beans, drained
2 tablespoons dried mixed herbs
large handful flat-leaf parsley, to garnish
8 tablespoons lowfat sour cream, to serve (optional)

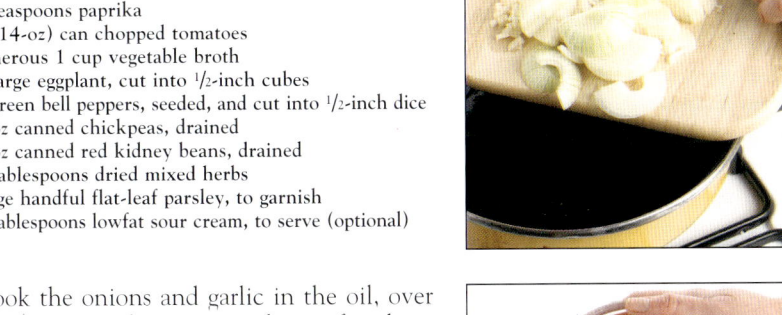

Cook the onions and garlic in the oil, over low heat in a large nonstick pan for about 10 minutes, until the onions have wilted and softened. Add the chili powder, cumin, and paprika and cook over medium heat for a couple of minutes before stirring in the tomatoes and vegetable broth. Bring to a boil over medium heat, stirring occasionally.

Add the eggplant, green bell pepper, chickpeas, red kidney beans, and dried mixed herbs to the pan. Stir, bring back to a boil, reduce heat, cover, and cook for 20 minutes to let the flavors infuse. Spoon into individual bowls and garnish with parsley before serving. Top with sour cream, if using.

Serves 8

CHICKPEA & EGGPLANT STEW

generous 1⅛ cups dried chickpeas, soaked overnight
1 teaspoon cumin seeds
2 teaspoons coriander seeds
2 tablespoons sesame seeds
2 teaspoons dried oregano
scant ¼ cup shelled Brazil nuts or almonds, toasted
3 tablespoons olive oil
2 onions, chopped
2 garlic cloves, minced
½ teaspoon chili powder, to taste
1 (14-oz) can chopped tomatoes
1 red bell pepper, diced
1 eggplant, cut into ¾-inch pieces
8 oz green beans, chopped
2½ cups vegetable broth
salt, to taste

3 tablespoons finely chopped fresh cilantro
plain yogurt, to serve

Drain the chickpeas and cook in boiling water for 20–30 minutes, until soft. Dry-fry the seeds together in a heavy-bottom pan until aromatic. Add the oregano and fry for a few more seconds. Put the seeds, oregano, and nuts in a blender and grind to a powder. Heat the oil in a Dutch oven. Add the onion and fry for 10 minutes, until translucent. Add the garlic, ground seed mixture, and chili powder.

Stir-fry for 2 minutes. Add the tomatoes, chickpeas, remaining vegetables, and the broth. Bring to a boil, season with salt, then cover and let simmer for 1 hour. Check the seasoning, adding more salt or chili powder if necessary. Stir in the cilantro and serve with yogurt.

Serves 6

RATATOUILLE

salt and pepper, to taste
2 eggplants, sliced and scored on both sides
4–6 zucchini, depending on size
3–6 tablespoons olive oil
2 onions, peeled and thinly sliced
2 green bell peppers, seeded and cut into 1-inch pieces
1 large garlic clove, minced
2 lb ripe tomatoes, peeled and quartered
2 teaspoons chopped fresh basil or 1 teaspoon dried basil
$1/2$ cup dry white wine

Salt the eggplant slices and place on paper towels for 20 minutes. Rinse and pat dry.

Slice the zucchini thickly and set them aside. Pour 3 tablespoons of the olive oil into a large skillet and when hot, lightly brown the onions, green bell peppers, and zucchini slices. Remove the vegetables to a Dutch oven and add the eggplant slices to the skillet or pan. Cook to brown both sides lightly and place in the Dutch oven with the other vegetables. Add extra oil as needed. Add the garlic and tomatoes and cook for 1 minute.

Add the garlic and tomatoes to the rest of the vegetables along with any remaining oil in the skillet. Add basil, salt, pepper, and wine and bring to a boil over medium heat. Cover and reduce to simmering. When the vegetables are tender, remove them from the casserole to a serving dish and boil any remaining liquid in the pan rapidly to reduce to about 2 tablespoons. Pour over the ratatouille to serve.

Serves 6–8

POTATO & BEAN STEW

1 1/3 cups dried cannellini or navy beans, soaked overnight and drained
3 tablespoons canola oil
1 lb new potatoes, or old potatoes, cut into chunks
1 large onion, chopped
2 leeks, sliced
2 garlic cloves, chopped
1 teaspoon cumin seeds, crushed
1 teaspoon paprika
8 oz canned chopped tomatoes
2 tablespoons tomato paste
4 cups vegetable broth
2 tablespoons chopped fresh cilantro
salt and freshly ground black pepper, to taste
plain yogurt, to serve

Boil the beans with enough water to cover for 10 minutes. Meanwhile, heat the oil in a Dutch oven and cook the potatoes, onion, and leeks for about 10 minutes or until the potatoes are pale gold in color. Stir in the garlic, cumin, and paprika and cook for about 1 minute. Then add the tomatoes, tomato paste, and broth and bring to a boil.

Drain the beans and add to the Dutch oven. Cover and let simmer gently for about 1 1/2 hours or until the beans are tender. Finally, stir in the cilantro and seasoning and serve with the plain yogurt.

Serves 4

RAGOUT OF YOUNG VEGETABLES

½ cup butter
6 baby onions, halved lengthwise
2–3 fresh thyme sprigs
pinch of salt
1 lb small baby potatoes
15 baby carrots
4 baby patty pan squash, halved
½ lb green beans
8 baby zucchini
8 oz thin asparagus, cut into 2-inch lengths
6 oz sugar snap peas, or snow peas
2 tablespoons finely chopped mixed herbs
juice of 1 lemon
1 garlic clove, finely chopped
salt and freshly ground black pepper, to taste

Bring a large pan of salted water to a boil. Melt 2 tablespoons of the butter in a large sauté pan. Add the onions, thyme, ¾ cup water, and a pinch of salt. Bring to a boil, cover, and simmer for 5 minutes. Meanwhile, blanch the vegetables separately in the order listed, allowing 5 minutes for the potatoes, 2 each for the carrots and squash, and 1 minute each for the other vegetables. Make sure the water comes back to a boil before adding each one.

As each batch of vegetables is blanched, remove with a slotted spoon and add to the onions. Stir, cover, and continue to simmer. Add a little more water if the mixture becomes dry. When all the vegetables are in the pan, stir in the herbs, lemon juice, garlic, and remaining butter. Season with salt and pepper. Stir over high heat until the butter melts and the sauce thickens slightly.

Serves 6

THE BOOK OF

EXOTIC RICE STEW

4 oz carrots
4 oz kohlrabi
7 oz leeks
7 oz Napa cabbage
3 tablespoons sesame oil
1 red chili, seeded and finely chopped
2 tablespoons finely chopped fresh ginger
scant 8½ cups rich chicken broth
½ cup sake (rice wine) or dry sherry
4 teaspoons soy sauce
1⅛ cups long-grain rice
1 tablespoon chopped fresh cilantro
salt and freshly ground white pepper, to taste

Peel and slice the carrots and kohlrabi. Cut the slices into thin strips. Trim and wash the leeks and Napa cabbage. Cut the leeks and Napa cabbage into thin strips.

Heat the oil in a pan, and gently fry the carrot, kohlrabi, leek, Napa cabbage, chili, and ginger for 5 minutes. Add the broth, sake or sherry, and soy sauce. Stir in the rice and cilantro, and season with salt and pepper. Cover and simmer over low heat for 15–20 minutes, until the rice is cooked. Serve immediately.

Serves 4

CHILIES & STEWS

SICILIAN RATATOUILLE

vegetable oil, for deep-frying
1 eggplant, cut into small cubes
10 green olives, pitted
2 tablespoons olive oil
$1/2$ celery stalk, cut into small pieces
1 large onion, sliced
1 teaspoon capers
1 teaspoon chopped garlic
1 teaspoon chopped fresh parsley
3 large tomatoes, peeled, seeded, and coarsely chopped
salt and pepper, to taste

Fry the eggplants in moderately hot oil, about 325F (165C), taking care that they do not turn brown. Remove with a slotted spoon and drain on paper towels. Cut the pitted olives into thin circles. Heat the olive oil in a Dutch oven and cook the celery, onion, olives, capers, garlic, and parsley together for 1 minute.

Stir in the chopped tomato and fried eggplant and season with salt and pepper. Cook over gentle heat for approximately 30 minutes. Stir gently, from time to time, to prevent sticking.

Serves 4

TACOS

12 taco shells
BEEF FILLING:
1 tablespoon olive oil
1 lb ground beef
1 medium onion, chopped
2 teaspoons ground cumin
2 teaspoons chili powder
pinch of paprika
1 garlic clove, minced
salt and pepper
CHICKEN FILLING:
3 tablespoons butter or margarine
1 medium onion, chopped
1 small red bell pepper, chopped
2 tablespoons slivered almonds
12 oz chicken breasts, skinned and finely chopped

salt and pepper
1 piece of fresh ginger, peeled and chopped
6 tablespoons milk
2 teaspoons cornstarch
$^2/_3$ cup sour cream
TOPPINGS:
shredded lettuce
grated cheese
tomatoes, seeded and chopped
chopped scallions
avocado slices
sour cream
jalapeño chilies, chopped
Taco Sauce (see page 16)

Preheat oven to 350F (180C). Heat the oil for the beef filling in a large skillet and brown the beef and onion, breaking the meat up with a fork as it cooks. Add the spices, garlic, salt, and pepper and cook for about 20 minutes. Set aside. Melt 2 tablespoons of the butter for the chicken filling in a medium pan and add the onion. Cook slowly until softened. Add the red bell pepper and almonds and cook slowly, until the almonds are lightly browned. Stir often during cooking. Remove to a plate and set aside.

CHILIES & STEWS

Melt the remaining butter in the same pan and cook the chicken for about 5 minutes, turning frequently. Season with salt and pepper and return the onion mixture to the pan along with the chopped ginger. Blend the milk and cornstarch together and stir into the chicken mixture. Bring to a boil and stir until very thick. Mix in the sour cream and cook gently to heat through. Do not boil.

Place the taco shells on a baking sheet, open end down, and heat in the oven for 2–3 minutes or according to the instructions on the package.

To fill, hold a taco shell in one hand and spoon in about 1 tablespoon of either beef or chicken filling. Next, add a layer of shredded lettuce, followed by a layer of grated cheese. Add choice of other toppings and finally spoon on some taco sauce. Serve immediately.

Makes 12

THE BOOK OF

TOSTADAS

2 teaspoons olive oil
2 teaspoons chili powder
1 teaspoon ground cumin
1 teaspoon ground coriander
1 lb ground beef or pork
8 oz canned refried beans
1 package (12) tostada shells
TOPPINGS:
shredded lettuce
grated cheddar or Jack cheese
tomatoes, seeded and chopped
sour cream
olives
shrimp, cooked
Taco Sauce (see page 16)

Heat the oil in a medium skillet, sprinkle with the spices, add meat, and cook for around 15 minutes. Reheat the beans. Place the taco shells on a baking sheet, open end down, and heat in the oven for 2–3 minutes or according to the instructions on the package.

Spread 1–2 tablespoons of the beans on each tostada shell. Top each shell with some of the beef mixture. Add layers of the remaining topping ingredients as desired and serve immediately.

Makes 12

CHILIES & STEWS

NACHOS

1¼ cups Taco Sauce (see page 16)
2 teaspoons vegetable oil
1 cup ground beef
2 teaspoons chili powder
pinch of ground coriander
pinch of cayenne pepper
salt and pepper, to taste
8 oz canned refried beans
1 package round tortilla chips
1 (about 8-oz) can jalapeño bean dip
8–10 cherry tomatoes, sliced
⅔ cup sour cream or plain yogurt
black and stuffed green olives, sliced, to serve
grated cheddar cheese, to serve

Prepare the Taco Sauce. Heat the oil in a large skillet over medium heat. Add the beef and brown, breaking the meat up with a fork as it cooks. Add the spices and seasoning and cook for about 15 minutes. Meanwhile, reheat the refried beans.

Top half of the tortilla chips with beans and a spoonful of Taco Sauce. Top the other half of the tortilla chips with the beef filling and spoonful of jalapeño bean dip. You can use either topping on either base if you want to mix things up. Top the tortilla chips with tomatoes, sour cream, or yogurt, olives, or cheese in any combination, and serve.

Serves 8–10

EMPANADAS

⅓ cup raisins
1 tablespoon apple cider vinegar
1 lb 2 oz ground beef
1 small onion, finely chopped
2 garlic cloves, finely chopped
generous 1 cup ready-made salsa
¼ cup slivered almonds
2 tablespoons packed brown sugar
½ teaspoon ground cinnamon
¼ teaspoon salt
1 lb 2 oz puff pastry or unsweetened pie dough, thawed if frozen
½ cup grated cheddar or Jack cheese
1 egg, lightly beaten

Preheat oven to 375F (190C). Mix raisins and vinegar in small bowl and let soak for 15–20 minutes or until raisins are plump. Meanwhile, cook the beef, onion, and garlic in a large skillet until the meat is well browned. Drain well and return to the heat. Add half the salsa, almonds, raisins, sugar, cinnamon, and salt. Bring to a boil and simmer for 3–4 minutes or until slightly thickened. Let cool.

Divide pastry or dough into 6 pieces. On well-floured board, roll each piece into an 8-inch circle. Divide the meat filling evenly among the circles. Sprinkle with the cheese. Fold top half of dough over filling and crimp the edges with the tines of a fork. Pierce top with a fork. Place on a greased baking sheet and brush with the egg. Bake for 20–25 minutes or until golden. Serve with remaining salsa.

Makes 6

BEEF & ORANGE CHILI

2 tablespoons vegetable oil
2¼ lb stewing beef, cut into chunks
2 large onions, coarsely chopped
2 green chilies, seeded and finely chopped
3 garlic cloves, minced
2 teaspoons dried oregano
finely grated zest ½ orange
2 (14-oz) cans chopped tomatoes
1 tablespoon chili sauce
3 tablespoons tomato paste
salt and freshly ground black pepper, to taste
1 (15-oz) can red kidney beans

Heat the oil in a Dutch oven. Add the beef cubes in batches and brown over high heat. Remove to a plate and set aside. Add the onions, chilies, and garlic to the pan and cook for about 5–6 minutes, until softened and starting to brown.

Return the beef to the pan and add the dried oregano, orange zest, tomatoes, chili sauce, and tomato paste. Season with salt and pepper and bring to the boil. Cover and let simmer for 1 hour. Add the beans and continue to simmer for a further ½ hour. Taste and season with salt and pepper if liked and serve hot.

Serves 4

RANCH CHILI

1 1/3 cups dried kidney beans
4 cups water
2 tablespoons vegetable oil
14 oz ground beef
3 onions, diced
1–4 small dried red chilies (depending on taste)
1 1/4 cups chicken broth
1 (14-oz) can chopped tomatoes or tomatillos
1 red bell pepper, seeded
2 garlic cloves, finely chopped
1/2 teaspoon dried oregano
1/2 teaspoon ground cumin
1/2 teaspoon salt
1/2 teaspoon chili powder

Place the dried beans in a bowl and pour over the water. Set aside overnight to soak. Drain the beans and then add to a pan of fresh water. Bring to a boil and boil vigorously for 15 minutes. Reduce the heat and cook for 1 1/2–2 hours, until they are almost soft. Heat the oil in a pan, and fry the beef and onions for 5–8 minutes. Cut the dried chilies into strips. Place them in a bowl, pour over the chicken broth, and set aside to soak. Drain and chop the tomatoes. Stir the tomatoes into the ground beef.

Cut the bell pepper into strips. Stir the chilies, pepper, garlic, oregano, cumin, salt, and chili powder into the ground beef mixture. Cook in an uncovered pan over a low heat for about 2 hours. Drain the beans, add and simmer for a further 30 minutes.

Serves 4

CHILIES & STEWS

CHILI ROJA

4 tablespoons vegetable oil
2 lb beef chuck steak, cut into 1-inch pieces
1 large red onion, coarsely chopped
2 garlic cloves, minced
2 red bell peppers, cut into 1-inch pieces
1 red chili, seeded and finely chopped
1–2 tablespoons mild chili powder
1 tablespoon ground cumin
1 tablespoon paprika
3½ cups beer, water, or broth
1 cup canned tomatoes, pureed
2 tablespoons tomato paste
1 cup canned red kidney beans, drained (about 8 oz)
salt, to taste
6 ripe tomatoes, peeled, seeded, and diced

Heat the oil in a Dutch oven. Add the meat in small batches and brown over medium-high heat for about 5 minutes per batch. Set aside the meat on a plate. Reduce the heat and cook the onion, garlic, red bell peppers, and chili for about 5 minutes. Add the chili powder, cumin, and paprika and cook for 1 minute.

Pour on the liquid and add the canned tomatoes, tomato paste, and the meat. Cover the Dutch oven and cook slowly for about 1½–2 hours. Add the beans about 45 minutes before the end of cooking time. When the meat is completely tender, add salt, and serve garnished with the diced tomatoes.

Serves 6–8

BEEF & PEPPER STEW

1 lb fillet of beef, cut into 1 inch strips
4–5 tablespoons vegetable oil
2 green bell peppers, thickly sliced
1 medium onion, sliced
2 scallions, chopped
1-inch fresh ginger, peeled and chopped
2 garlic cloves, chopped
3 green chilies, seeded and chopped
MARINADE:
2 tablespoons dark soy sauce
1 teaspoon sesame oil
$1/4$ teaspoon ground black pepper
$1/2$ teaspoon salt
SAUCE:
2 tablespoons chicken broth
1 teaspoon dark soy sauce

salt, to taste
few drops of sesame oil

Mix together the marinade ingredients in a self-sealing plastic bag, add the beef, and let marinate for 15 minutes. Meanwhile, heat 2 tablespoons of the oil in a preheated wok and stir-fry the green bell peppers, onion, and scallions for 2 minutes. Remove to a plate.

Reheat the wok, add the remaining oil, and fry the ginger, garlic, and green chilies for 1 minute. Add the beef and stir-fry for 4–5 minutes. Add the sauce ingredients, mixed together, and the fried bell peppers and onion. Stir-fry for 2 minutes and serve.

Serves 4

CHILIES & STEWS

QUICK & EASY CHILI

1 tablespoon vegetable oil
1 lb ground beef
2 teaspoons ground cumin
2 teaspoons mild or hot chili powder
pinch of dried oregano
salt and freshly ground black pepper, to taste
pinch of sugar
1 teaspoon minced garlic
2 tablespoons all-purpose flour
3 cups canned chopped tomatoes (about 24 oz)
1 (15-oz) can red kidney beans

Heat the oil in a large pan and brown the meat, breaking it up with a fork as it cooks. Sprinkle on the cumin, chili powder, oregano, salt, pepper, sugar, garlic, and flour.

Cook, stirring frequently, over medium heat for about 3 minutes. Add the tomatoes and their liquid and let simmer 25–30 minutes. Drain the kidney beans and add just before serving. Heat through for about 5 minutes.

Serves 4

BEEF STROGANOFF

1 lb 2 oz fillet of beef
3 tablespoons sunflower oil
1 tablespoon butter
2 small onions, chopped
5½ oz mushrooms, thinly sliced
3 tablespoons white wine
1 gherkin
½ cup crème fraîche or sour cream
1 teaspoon English mustard
salt and freshly ground black pepper, to taste

Cut the beef into short, thick strips. Heat the oil in a skillet and fry the meat. The strips should remain pink in the middle.

Remove the meat from the skillet and keep warm. Add the butter to the skillet, and melt. Add the onions and fry until transparent. Add the mushrooms and fry for 2–3 minutes. Add the wine.

Thinly slice the gherkin and add to the skillet. Mix together the crème fraîche and mustard, add to the pan, bring to a boil, and allow to reduce a little. Return the meat to the skillet and heat through. Season to taste with salt and pepper.

Serves 4

HUNTER'S STEW

4 tablespoons vegetable oil
1 onion, thickly sliced
2 garlic cloves, minced
¾ lb beef round or pork shoulder, cut into 2-inch pieces
4 tablespoons all-purpose flour
2 tablespoons mild paprika
4 cups light broth
4 oz smoked ham, cut into 2-inch pieces
4 oz smoked sausage, cut into 2-inch pieces
1 teaspoon dried marjoram
1 teaspoon chopped fresh thyme
1 teaspoon chopped fresh parsley
salt and pepper, to taste
2 tablespoons tomato paste
1 head white cabbage, chopped

2 apples, cored and chopped
2 carrots, thinly sliced
8 pitted prunes, coarsely chopped
3 tomatoes, peeled and coarsely chopped
⅓ cup red wine or Madeira
pinch of sugar (optional)

Heat the oil in a Dutch oven. Add the onion and garlic and cook for 2–3 minutes. Remove and set aside. Add the steak in four small batches, cooking over a high heat to brown. Return it to the Dutch oven with the onion and garlic, sprinkle over flour, and cook, until light brown.

Add paprika and cook for 1–2 minutes. Pour broth in gradually and bring to a boil. Reduce heat and add smoked meat, herbs, salt, pepper, and tomato paste. Stir well, cover, and cook over low heat for 45 minutes. Add more liquid if necessary. When the meat is almost tender, add the cabbage, apples, carrots, and prunes. Cook for 20 minutes. Add the tomatoes, wine or Madeira, and a pinch of sugar, if desired. Cook for 10 minutes, add salt and pepper, and serve.

Serves 8

HUNGARIAN VEAL GOULASH

2 small red bell peppers
4 onions
2 slices lean raw ham
2 tablespoons vegetable oil
14 oz boneless veal, cubed
salt and freshly ground black pepper, to taste
1 tablespoon sweet paprika
1 teaspoon fresh chopped marjoram
2 cups meat broth
2 tablespoons sour cream
1 tablespoon fresh minced parsley

Halve, seed, wash, and chop the bell peppers. Peel and chop the onions. Chop the ham into $1/2$-inch cubes.

Heat the oil in a Dutch oven, and fry the onions, bell peppers, and ham for 5 minutes over medium heat. Add the veal, and season with salt, pepper, paprika, and marjoram. Mix thoroughly and fry for another 5 minutes, stirring occasionally.

Add the broth, cover, and let simmer for 30 minutes. Stir in the sour cream, heat through, and garnish the goulash with parsley. Serve with boiled potatoes or noodles and a green salad.

Serves 4

BEEF STEW

2½ lb chuck or round steak
3 tablespoons vegetable oil
2 onions
2 small turnips, diced
3 carrots, diced
3 potatoes, diced
2 celery stalks, sliced
½ cup all-purpose flour
½ teaspoon salt
¼ teaspoon black pepper
4 cups water
1 bay leaf
1 cup fresh or frozen peas

Cut meat into 2-inch pieces, trimming off the fat. Heat the oil in a large pan and fry the meat in small batches, until well browned. Remove and set aside. Add the onions, turnips, carrots, potatoes, and celery to the pan and cook slowly to brown lightly. Remove and set aside with the meat, leaving the "juice." If necessary, add more oil to the pan. Add the flour and cook slowly, until a good, rich brown color.

Return the meat and vegetables to the pan and add the salt, pepper, water, and bay leaf. Bring to a boil, then reduce the heat and let simmer for about 2 hours or until the meat and vegetables are tender. Remove the bay leaf and add the peas to the stew. Cook for about 15 minutes or until peas are tender.

Serves 4–6

RAGOUT LA BERGHOFF

¾ cup butter
3½ lb boneless round steak, cut into thin strips
1 cup chopped onion
1½ cups chopped green bell pepper
1 lb mushrooms, sliced
½ cup all-purpose flour
2 cups beef broth
1 cup dry white wine
1 teaspoon salt
1 teaspoon Worcestershire sauce
few drops Tabasco sauce, to taste

Melt ½ cup of the butter in large skillet. Add the meat and brown over medium-high heat. Remove the browned meat to a plate.

Add the onion to the skillet and sauté for 2 minutes. Add the green bell pepper and mushrooms and cook for another 3 minutes. Set aside.

Melt the remaining ¼ cup butter and add the flour. Slowly add the beef broth and cook until thickened. Stir in the wine, salt, and Worcestershire and Tabasco sauces. Add the meat and mushroom mixtures. Cover and let simmer for 45 minutes–1 hour, until the meat is tender.

Serves 8

CHILIES & STEWS

TUSCANY BEEF

all-purpose flour, for dredging
2 lb top round steak, cut into small cubes
3 tablespoons olive oil
1 garlic clove, chopped
1/2 teaspoon chopped fresh rosemary
scant 2 1/2 cups red wine
2 tablespoons tomato paste
salt and pepper, to taste

Put some flour on a plate and toss the meat cubes in the flour. Heat the oil in a Dutch oven, add the garlic, meat, and rosemary. Fry on all sides, until the meat is well browned.

Deglaze the Dutch oven with the red wine, and then pour in just enough water to cover the meat. Stir in the tomato paste, season with salt and pepper, cover, and let simmer gently for approximately 2 hours.

Check the level of the liquid during cooking and add water if necessary. Check the meat for tenderness and remove from the heat when cooked through. Serve with mashed potatoes and asparagus.

Serves 4

RAGOUT BOLOGNESE

2 tablespoons olive oil
1 large onion, finely chopped
1 medium carrot, finely chopped
1 celery stalk, finely chopped
¼ cup chopped bacon
1 lb 2 oz ground beef
⅔ cup red wine
1¼ cups beef broth
1 tablespoon tomato paste
⅔ cup heavy cream
salt and freshly ground black pepper, to taste

Heat the olive oil in a large pan. Add the onion, carrot, and celery and cook gently for about 10 minutes, until softened.

Add the bacon and ground beef and cook over high heat for another 10–12 minutes, until well browned. Drain any excess fat from the pan. Add the red wine and simmer rapidly, until reduced and syrupy.

Stir in about half the beef broth along with the tomato paste. Simmer, covered, for 1–1½ hours, adding the beef broth as necessary to keep the mixture moist—you may not need all of it. Just before serving, stir in the heavy cream and season with salt and pepper. Serve with tagliatelle or other pasta shapes.

Serves 4

PIEDMONT BEEF STEW

1 cup chicken broth
1 cup water
1 lb lean shoulder of beef
1 large smoked sausage (or a few small ones)
8 oz loin of veal
3 carrots
½ leek, thinly sliced
1 onion, stuck with 1 clove
4 juniper berries
1 bay leaf
1 bouquet garni
salt and pepper, to taste
2 zucchini

Heat the broth in a Dutch oven.

Add the water and the beef, sausage, and veal. Add 1 carrot, cut into circles, and the leek, onion, juniper berries, bay leaf, and bouquet garni. Season with salt and pepper, add more water to completely cover, and let simmer for 2½ hours. Meanwhile, cut the remaining carrots and the zucchini into oval slices and steam for a few minutes—they should still be quite crisp.

When the stew is cooked, remove the meat with a slotted spoon. Slice the beef thinly and place on a warmed serving dish. Cut the sausage into circles and cut the meat and fat off the veal into small cubes. Add to the beef. Strain the juices into a clean pan through a very fine strainer. Add the steamed vegetables to the pan and heat through before serving.

Serves 4

ENCHILADAS

10 ripe tomatoes, peeled, seeded, and chopped
1 small onion, chopped
1–2 green or red chilies, seeded and chopped
1 garlic clove, minced
pinch each of salt and sugar
1–2 tablespoons tomato paste
2 tablespoons butter or margarine
2 eggs
1 1/4 cups heavy cream
1 1/2 cups ground pork
4 tablespoons raisins
4 tablespoons pine nuts
1 small red bell pepper, chopped
salt and pepper, to taste
12 corn tortillas
4 tablespoons grated cheese

Place the tomatoes, onion, chilies, garlic, salt, sugar, and tomato paste in a blender and purée until smooth. Melt the butter in a large pan, add the purée and simmer for 5 minutes. Beat together the eggs and cream. Add a spoonful of the hot tomato purée to the cream and eggs and mix quickly. Return to the pan and heat slowly, stirring, until the mixture thickens. Do not boil. Meanwhile, cook the pork slowly in a large skillet. Use a fork to break up the meat. Increase the heat when the pork is nearly cooked and fry briskly for a few minutes.

Add the raisins, pine nuts, bell pepper, and seasoning. Combine a quarter of the sauce with the meat and divide the mixture evenly among all the tortillas. Spoon on the filling and roll up the tortilla, leaving the ends open. Place the enchiladas in a baking dish and pour over the remaining sauce. Sprinkle over the cheese and bake in an oven preheated to 350F (180C) for 15–20 minutes. Serve immediately.

Serves 6

CHORIZO & POTATO CHILI

1¾ cups ground pork
2 onions, 1 cut into wedges and the other grated finely
2 teaspoons ground cumin
1 teaspoon dried chili flakes
2 tablespoons canola oil
1 cup celery or fennel bulb, sliced
5 cups new potatoes, halved if large
2 cups chorizo sausage, coarsely chopped
2 (14-oz) cans chopped tomatoes
1 (15-oz) can navy or cannellini beans, drained and rinsed
salt and freshly ground black pepper, to taste

In a bowl, mix together the ground pork, grated onion, cumin, and chili flakes. Shape into 16 walnut-size balls. Heat the oil in a large heavy-bottom pan. Add the meatballs and brown. Set the meatballs aside and drain any excess fat from the pan, leaving behind about 1 tablespoon. Add the onion wedges and celery to the same pan and cook for about 10 minutes, until softened and browned.

Return the meatballs to the pan with the remaining ingredients. Cover and let simmer over gentle heat for 35 minutes or until potatoes are tender and the sauce has thickened.

Serves 6

SAUSAGE CHILI

2 tablespoons olive oil
1 large onion, chopped
1 lb 2 oz spicy sausages
1–2 garlic cloves, minced (if the sausages are garlicky, use less)
1 red bell pepper, seeded and thinly sliced
1 tablespoon chili powder
1 teaspoon ground cumin
1 (15-oz) can red kidney beans, drained and rinsed
1 (14-oz) can chopped tomatoes
1 bay leaf
salt and freshly ground black pepper, to taste

Heat the oil in a large skillet and add the onion. Cook for 5 minutes, until softened.

Remove the sausage skins by slitting the skin and unwrapping the meat. Add the meat to the pan and cook over high heat, breaking up the meat with a wooden spoon. Allow the meat to brown. Drain off any excess fat.

Add the garlic and bell pepper and continue cooking until the pepper is softened. Add the chili powder and cumin and stir well before adding the beans, tomatoes, and bay leaf. Bring to a boil and simmer gently for about 1 hour. Discard the bay leaf. Season with salt and pepper and serve hot with rice or warmed tortillas.

Serves 4

PORK & LIME CHILI

1 garlic clove, minced
1 teaspoon brown sugar
1 teaspoon olive oil
1 teaspoon lime juice
1 teaspoon cornstarch
1 lb lean pork, cut into 1-inch cubes
²/₃ cup vegetable oil, for deep-frying
1 green chili, seeded and thinly sliced
1 red chili, seeded and thinly sliced
8 scallions, trimmed and diagonally sliced
1 teaspoon each turmeric, ground coriander, ground cumin, and ground nutmeg
pinch of ground cloves
4 tablespoons soy sauce
grated zest and juice of 1 lime
²/₃ cup coconut milk
salt and pepper, to taste

Combine the garlic, sugar, olive oil, 1 teaspoon lime juice, and cornstarch in a large bowl. Stir in the cubed pork and coat thoroughly with the garlic and lime juice mixture. Let stand in the refrigerator for at least 1 hour. Heat the oil for frying in a wok and add the pork cubes. Cook, stirring frequently, for about 10 minutes, until golden brown and cooked through. Drain and set aside.

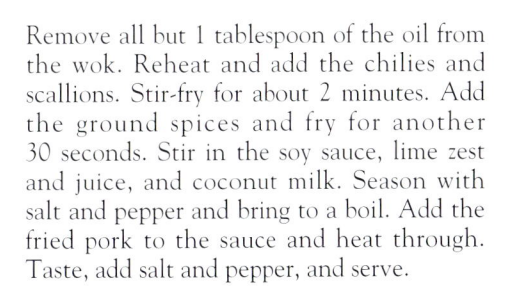

Remove all but 1 tablespoon of the oil from the wok. Reheat and add the chilies and scallions. Stir-fry for about 2 minutes. Add the ground spices and fry for another 30 seconds. Stir in the soy sauce, lime zest and juice, and coconut milk. Season with salt and pepper and bring to a boil. Add the fried pork to the sauce and heat through. Taste, add salt and pepper, and serve.

Serves 4

PORK RIB CHILI

2 tablespoons vegetable or olive oil
2¼ lb pork ribs, chopped into 2-inch pieces
1 large onion, finely chopped
1 carrot, chopped
1 green bell pepper, seeded and finely chopped
2 tablespoons chili powder
2 teaspoons dried oregano
½ teaspoon dried chili flakes
1 (15-oz) can mixed beans or pinto beans, drained and rinsed
1 (14-oz) can chopped tomatoes
1 teaspoon sugar
salt and freshly ground black pepper, to taste

Heat the oil in a large pan. Add the pork ribs in batches and brown. Remove to a plate and set aside. Add the onion, carrot, and green bell pepper to the pan and cook for about 8–10 minutes, until golden. Return the ribs to the pan along with the chili powder, oregano, and chili flakes. Stir well and cook for another minute before adding the tomatoes and sugar.

Bring to a boil and let simmer, covered, for 1 hour. Remove the cover, add the beans, and continue to cook gently for another 30 minutes, until the ribs are meltingly tender and the sauce has thickened. Season with salt and pepper.

Serves 4

CHILI VERDE

- 4 tablespoons olive oil
- 2 lb lean pork, cut into 1-inch pieces
- 3 green bell peppers, cut into 1-inch pieces
- 1–2 green chilies, seeded and finely chopped
- 1 small bunch scallions, chopped
- 2 garlic cloves, minced
- 2 teaspoons chopped fresh oregano
- 3 tablespoons chopped fresh cilantro
- 1 bay leaf
- $3^{1}/_{2}$ cups beer, water, or chicken broth
- 1 cup canned chickpeas, drained (about 8 oz)
- $1^{1}/_{2}$ tablespoons cornstarch mixed with 3 tablespoons cold water (optional)
- salt and pepper, to taste
- 1 large ripe avocado
- 1 tablespoon lemon or lime juice

Heat oil in a Dutch oven and lightly brown the pork cubes in 2–3 batches over high heat. Reduce the heat and cook the bell peppers to soften slightly. Add the chilies, scallions, and garlic and cook for 2 minutes. Add the herbs and beer and reduce the heat. Let simmer, covered, for $1^{1}/_{2}$ hours or until the meat is tender.

Add the chickpeas during the last 45 minutes. If necessary, thicken with cornstarch, stirring constantly after adding, until the liquid thickens and clears. Add salt and pepper and remove the bay leaf. Peel and slice the avocado then quickly toss in the lemon juice and serve with the chili.

Serves 6–8

PORK & CHOCOLATE CHILI

3 tablespoons vegetable oil
1 lb 2 oz pork fillet, cut into large chunks
1 onion, chopped
1 small green and 1 small red bell pepper, chopped
3 garlic cloves, chopped
1 1/2 tablespoons chili powder
2 tomatoes, chopped
2 1/2 cups chicken broth
1/2 cup slivered almonds
pinch each of ground cumin, ground nutmeg, ground cinnamon, and ground cloves
2 tablespoons chopped fresh cilantro
2 tablespoons raisins
pinch of sugar
grated zest of 1/2 orange
1 oz semisweet chocolate, coarsely chopped or grated

salt and freshly ground black pepper, to taste

Heat the oil in a large pan or ovenproof casserole. Add the pork and fry until browned on all sides. Remove the browned pork to a plate and set aside. Add the onion, red and green bell peppers, and garlic to the pan. Cook over medium heat, stirring often, until softened. Add the chili powder and cook another minute before adding the tomatoes.

Return the pork to the pan and pour in the broth, slivered almonds, spices, and cilantro and bring to a boil. Let cook for 5 minutes, stirring now and then, until the sauce has reduced and thickened. Stir in the raisins, sugar, and orange zest. Return the pork to the pan, cover the dish with a lid, and let simmer gently for 1 hour or until the pork is cooked through. Stir the chocolate into the sauce until melted and smooth. Season with salt and pepper and serve.

Serves 4

SPICED PORK & CORN CHILI

1½ lb pork loin
3 tablespoons vegetable oil
3 garlic cloves
1 large onion
2 green or red chilies
2½ cups canned tomatoes, chopped
1 cup canned corn kernels
1 fresh thyme sprig
salt and freshly ground black pepper, to taste

Rinse the pork and pat dry. Cut into ¾-inch cubes. Heat the oil and fry the pork, in batches, until brown. Peel and mince the garlic. Peel and chop the onion.

Add the garlic and onion to the pan, and fry for another 5 minutes. Halve, seed, and wash the chilies. Cut into thin rings and add to the pan. Stir in the tomatoes with their juice. Cover and cook for 10 minutes.

Drain the corn and add to the pan, along with the thyme, cover, and cook for another 10 minutes. Season with salt and pepper. Remove and discard thyme before serving.

Serves 4

PORK & BEAN CHILI

2 tablespoons vegetable oil
2 lb slab pork belly (fresh bacon) or streak of lean
   (if not available substitute 4 lb spareribs), cut into
   2-inch chunks
2 large garlic cloves, minced
2 yellow bell peppers, cored, seeded, and chopped
1 fresh jalapeño chili, seeded and finely chopped
1 large onion, chopped
2 tablespoons tomato paste
1 (14-oz) can chopped tomatoes
vegetable broth or water
3 tablespoons dark brown sugar
1 tablespoon Worcestershire sauce
salt and freshly ground black pepper, to taste
2 (15-oz) cans pinto beans, drained and rinsed
hot pepper sauce (optional)

Heat the oil in a Dutch oven over medium heat. Add the pork and fry, stirring, for about 5 minutes, until browned. Add the garlic, bell pepper, jalapeño chili, and onion and continue cooking, stirring, for about 5 minutes longer, until just softened. Stir in the tomato paste, tomatoes with their juice, and enough broth or water to cover.

Bring to a boil, then reduce the heat, cover the pan, and let simmer gently for about 45 minutes, stirring the mixture occasionally. Stir in the sugar, Worcestershire sauce, and salt and pepper. Add the canned beans and several drops of hot pepper sauce for a hot, spicy mixture. Leave the pot uncovered and continue to simmer for 15 minutes, until the beans are very tender.

Serves 4–6

THAI PORK CHILI

3 tablespoons dried Chinese mushrooms
1 onion
1 garlic clove
2 green chilies
3 tablespoons vegetable oil
1 cup ground pork
1 tablespoon finely chopped fresh ginger
1 1/4 cups coconut milk
5 oz cooked shrimp, shelled
1 tablespoon soy sauce
2 tablespoons Thai fish sauce
1/2 teaspoon sugar
salt, to taste
1 tablespoon chopped fresh cilantro leaves

Rinse the mushrooms, place in a bowl, cover with hot water, and set aside to soak for about 10 minutes. Drain well and reserve the soaking liquid. Peel and finely chop the onion and garlic. Seed the chilies. Heat the oil in a preheated wok or skillet, and stir-fry the ground pork. Add the ginger, garlic, and onion, and stir-fry until the onion begins to color. Stir in the mushrooms and the chilies, and fry for another 4 minutes.

Strain the mushroom soaking liquid through a fine strainer and combine with the coconut milk. Stir the liquid into the pork-and-onion mixture, and heat through. Add the shrimp, and return the liquid to a boil. Add the soy sauce, fish sauce, sugar and, if necessary, season with a little salt. Serve garnished with chopped cilantro leaves. Serve with rice.

Serves 4

LEEK & PORK STEW

1 lb 2 oz potatoes
1 lb 2 oz leeks
2 tablespoons vegetable oil
4 cups meat broth
1 lb pork fillet
1 teaspoon dried marjoram
salt and freshly ground black pepper, to taste
1 tablespoon red wine vinegar

Peel the potatoes and chop into 1/2-inch cubes. Trim and wash the leeks, and slice into 1/4-inch rings. Heat the oil in a pan, add the pork and brown for 5 minutes. Remove from the pan and put aside.

Add the potatoes and leeks to the pan and fry for 5 minutes. Add the broth and bring to a boil. Cover, reduce the heat, and let simmer for 25 minutes. Meanwhile, cut the pork into 1/2-inch cubes. Stir the pork into the vegetables.

Sprinkle over the marjoram, and season with salt and pepper. Simmer for another 10 minutes. Stir in the vinegar. Serve hot.

Serves 4

CHILIES & STEWS

CURRIED PORK STEW

- 2 tablespoons olive oil
- 2 lb pork shoulder, cut into 2-inch cubes
- 2 medium onions, cut into 2-inch pieces
- ½ green bell pepper, seeded and cut into 2-inch pieces
- ½ orange bell pepper, seeded and cut into 2-inch pieces
- 1 tablespoon curry powder
- 2 garlic cloves, minced
- 1 lb canned tomatoes
- 3 tablespoons tomato paste
- ⅔ cup water or beef broth
- 2 tablespoons cider vinegar
- 1 bay leaf
- ½ teaspoon dried mint
- salt and a few drops Tabasco sauce, to taste

Heat the oil in a large sauté pan or skillet. When hot, add the pork cubes in 2 batches. Brown over high heat for about 5 minutes per batch. Remove to a plate. Add more oil if necessary and add the onions and bell peppers; cook to soften slightly. Add the curry powder and garlic and cook for another minute. Add the tomatoes with their juice and the tomato paste. Stir in the water or broth and vinegar breaking up the tomatoes slightly. Add the bay leaf, mint, and salt.

Transfer to a Dutch oven. Bring the mixture to a boil and then cook slowly for about 1½ hours, covered. When the meat is completely tender, skim any fat from the surface of the sauce, remove the bay leaf, and add a few drops of Tabasco sauce.

Serves 4

IRISH STEW

about 2 lb lamb for stew
2¼ lb potatoes
4 large onions
salt and freshly ground black pepper, to taste
1 bay leaf
scant 2½ cups meat broth or water
1 tablespoon butter

Wash the meat and pat dry. Cut into chunks, if necessary. Peel and slice the potatoes and onions.

Place half the potato slices in the bottom of a large pan, cover with some of the sliced onion, and then with the meat, and the rest of the onion. Season generously with salt and pepper, finishing off with potato on top. Season with salt and pepper once more, add the bay leaf, and pour over the meat broth or water.

Grease one side of a sheet of aluminum foil or waxed paper with the butter and place it over the stew. Cover the pan tightly with a lid, and braise slowly over medium heat for about 1½ hours.

Serves 4

HAM & GREEN LENTIL RAGOUT

2½ lb ham
6 herb sausages
2 lb green lentils
1 large onion, stuck with 2 whole cloves
1 lb carrots, cut into chunks
1 bouquet garni
salt, to taste

Wash the ham under cold running water, place it in a large pan, and cover with cold water. Bring to a boil, reduce heat, and cook for 2 hours. After 2 hours, add the sausages to the pan, cook for 10 minutes, and then remove from the heat.

Set the lentils to cook in a large quantity of water with the onion, carrot, bouquet garni, and a little salt. Bring gently to a boil, reduce the heat, and let simmer for approximately 30–40 minutes.

After about 30 minutes, add the ham and the sausages and continue cooking until the lentils are cooked. Drain off a little of the liquid, if necessary, and remove the bouquet garni. Remove the meat and sausages, cut into chunks, return to pan, heat through again, and serve.

Serves 6

LEMON PORK RAGOUT

2½–3 lb boneless lean pork shoulder, cut into 2-inch pieces
2 teaspoons canola oil
2 teaspoons dried cumin
2 teaspoons ground coriander
1 teaspoon saffron powder
2 garlic cloves, minced
1 large onion, chopped
1 teaspoon whole wheat flour
1¾ cups broth
⅔ cup golden raisins
2 lemons, peeled, each cut into quarters, plus extra slices for serving
2 teaspoons grated lemon zest
6 fresh Italian plum tomatoes, quartered

Marinade the pork with the oil, cumin, coriander, saffron, and garlic in a shallow dish for about 20–30 minutes. In a large nonstick pan, sauté the pork pieces in small batches over medium-high heat. Remove with a slotted spoon and set aside in a bowl. Add the onion to the pan and sauté for 1–2 minutes over medium heat.

Sprinkle over the flour and add in the broth, golden raisins, lemon, lemon zest, and tomatoes. Return the meat to the pan. Stir, cover, and let simmer for 1½–2 hours, stirring occasionally and adding more broth if necessary. Serve with extra lemon slices on the side.

Serves 6

CHILIES & STEWS

TOMATO & CHICKPEA STEW

1 ⅛ cups dried chickpeas
2 lb leg of lamb, boned (ask your butcher for the bone for making broth)
1 bunch scallions
2 garlic cloves
1 red chili
2 ½–3 lb ripe beefsteak tomatoes
4 tablespoons olive oil
1 (14-oz) can chopped tomatoes, drained
salt, to taste
generous 6 ½ cups strong beef broth
2 tablespoons fresh torn basil leaves

Place the chickpeas in a bowl, cover with cold water, and set aside overnight to soak. Trim the lamb and cut into bite-size pieces, setting the bone aside. Trim, wash, and finely dice the scallions. Peel and finely dice the garlic. Halve, seed, and finely dice the chili. Wash and quarter the beefsteak tomatoes. Heat the oil in a large pan, add the lamb, and fry it on all sides for a few minutes over high heat. Remove the lamb, cover, and set aside. Add the lamb bone, onions, garlic, and chili to the pan, and fry for 5 minutes.

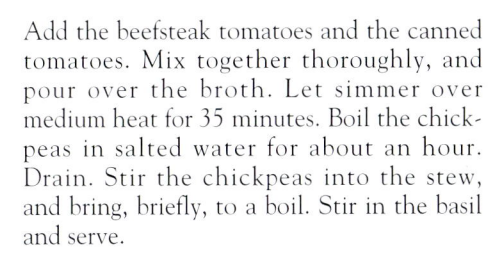

Add the beefsteak tomatoes and the canned tomatoes. Mix together thoroughly, and pour over the broth. Let simmer over medium heat for 35 minutes. Boil the chickpeas in salted water for about an hour. Drain. Stir the chickpeas into the stew, and bring, briefly, to a boil. Stir in the basil and serve.

Serves 4

THE BOOK OF

WELSH STEW

1 oz shortening
1½ lb neck of lamb or lamb shoulder roast, in one piece
2 onions, chopped
2 parsnips, peeled and cut into chunks
1 large turnip, peeled and cut into chunks
3–4 carrots, peeled and cut into thick slices
1 lb piece smoked ham, cubed
few peppercorns
1 bay leaf
1 fresh parsley sprig
1 fresh rosemary sprig
about 9 cups light broth or water
1 lb potatoes, peeled and cut into chunks
4 leeks, washed and thickly sliced

Melt the shortening in a skillet and fry the lamb on all sides until brown. Transfer to a Dutch oven. Add the onions, parsnips, turnip, and carrots and fry, in batches if necessary, until just beginning to soften. Add to the meat.

Remove any excess fat from the ham and add to the Dutch oven along with the peppercorns, bay leaf, parsley, and rosemary. Add the broth or water to cover.

CHILIES & STEWS

Bring gently to a boil and skim off any scum that rises to the surface. Reduce the heat, cover, and allow to simmer for 2–3 hours.

Add the potatoes to the Dutch oven. Add the leeks to the stew and cook for another 30 minutes, stirring occasionally to prevent sticking.

To serve, remove the meat and slice. Divide the meat among the serving bowls and then spoon over the vegetables and as much broth as desired.

Serves 8

LAMB RAGOUT

5 oz asparagus tips
6 oz baby zucchini
1½ lb boneless leg of lamb
juice of 2 lemons
salt and freshly ground black pepper, to taste
2 shallots
1 garlic clove
2 tablespoons vegetable oil
½ cup veal or vegetable broth
1 tablespoons minced fresh parsley

Clean and cut the asparagus tips in half. Trim the tops of the zucchini and diagonally cut into ½-inch pieces. Rinse the lamb and pat dry. Cut into 1-inch cubes, place in a shallow dish, cover with the juice of 1 of the lemons, season with salt and pepper and leave to marinade for 30 minutes. Peel and chop the shallots and garlic. Heat the oil, and fry the shallots and garlic until transparent. Add the marinated lamb and fry for 5 minutes, stirring frequently.

Stir in the broth, cover, and let simmer for about 30 minutes. Add the aparagus, zucchini, remaining lemon juice, and parsley and continue to cook for 10 minutes before serving.

Serves 4

FLAUTAS

1 tablespoon vegetable oil, plus extra for frying
8 oz chicken, skinned, boned, and ground or finely chopped
1 small onion, finely chopped
1/2 green bell pepper, finely chopped
1/2–1 chili, seeded and finely chopped
3/4 cup frozen corn kernels
6 black olives, pitted and chopped
1/2 cup heavy cream
salt, to taste
12 (8-inch) ready-made flour tortillas
Taco sauce (see page 16), guacamole, and sour cream, to serve

Heat the oil in a medium skillet and add the chicken, onion, and bell pepper. Cook over medium heat, stirring frequently to break up the pieces of chicken. When the chicken is cooked and the vegetables are softened, add the chili, corn, olives, cream, and salt. Bring to a boil and boil rapidly, stirring continuously, to reduce and thicken the cream. Place 2 tortillas side-by-side on a clean counter, overlapping them by about 2 inches. Spoon some of the chicken mixture in a line across the middle of the 2 tortillas, roll up the two together, and secure.

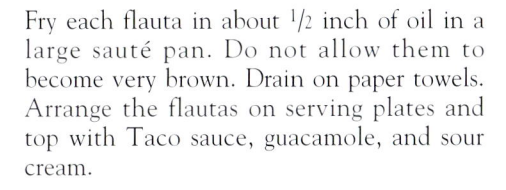

Fry each flauta in about 1/2 inch of oil in a large sauté pan. Do not allow them to become very brown. Drain on paper towels. Arrange the flautas on serving plates and top with Taco sauce, guacamole, and sour cream.

Serves 6

CHIMICHANGAS

2 tablespoons vegetable or olive oil
1 medium onion, chopped
2 garlic cloves, finely chopped
2 green chilies, seeded and finely chopped
1½ teaspoons dried oregano
1–2 teaspoons chili powder
2 medium tomatoes, chopped
generous ⅓ cup chicken broth
2 cups chopped or shredded cooked chicken
1 (15-oz) can pinto ot other beans, drained and rinsed
2 tablespoons chopped fresh cilantro
8 flour tortillas, warmed
vegetable oil, for pan-frying
TOPPINGS:
grated cheddar or Jack cheese
sour cream
guacamole
salsa
shredded lettuce, chopped tomatoes, sliced black olives

In a large skillet, heat the oil and add onion, garlic, and chilies. Cook for 7–8 minutes, until lightly golden. Add the oregano and chili powder and cook for another minute. Add the tomatoes, stirring to break them up, before adding the broth. Simmer for about 5 minutes, until thickened. Stir in the chicken and pinto beans until piping hot.

Remove from the heat and stir in the chopped fresh cilantro. Season with salt and pepper and set aside to cool slightly. Place a generous spoonful of the filling on each tortilla. Fold to create an envelope. Fry, seam side down, in ½ inch of hot oil, until crispy and brown. Turn and brown the other side. Drain briefly on paper towels. Place on plate and top with grated cheese, sour cream, guacamole, and salsa.

Makes 8 chimichangas

CHICKEN CHILI WITH TORTILLAS

2 tablespoons olive oil
2 onions, chopped
2 garlic cloves, minced
4 green chilies, seeded and finely chopped
3 tablespoons chopped fresh cilantro (plus the stalks reserved and finely chopped)
2 teaspoons ground cumin
1 (15-oz) can black eye peas, drained and rinsed
2½ cups chicken broth
1 teaspoon chili sauce
salt and freshly ground black pepper, to taste
2¼ lb skinless, boneless chicken thighs, cut into bite-size pieces
1 cup crushed tortilla chips
juice of ½ lime

Heat the oil in a Dutch oven over gentle heat, and cook the onions, garlic, chilies, and cilantro stalks for about 10 minutes, stirring once or twice, until softened. Add the ground cumin, along with the drained beans, to the Dutch oven and stir. Next, add the broth and chili sauce and a little salt. Bring everything to a simmer and cook, covered, on the lowest heat possible for about 1 hour, until the sauce begins to thicken. When the chili has had its initial cooking time, stir the chicken into the Dutch oven.

Season well with salt and black pepper, cover, and let simmer for another 30 minutes. Add the tortilla chips and stir well. Simmer for another 5 minutes before adding the lime juice and reserved chopped cilantro. Serve immediately.

Serves 4

CHINESE CHILI CHICKEN

1 tablespoon peanut oil
4 chicken breasts, sliced
1 medium onion, finely sliced
2 garlic cloves, finely chopped
1 teaspoon finely grated fresh ginger
½ yellow bell pepper
1 medium chili, seeded and finely chopped
1 tablespoon dark soy sauce
1 tablespoon white wine vinegar
1 tablespoon dry sherry or rice wine
1½ tablespoons chili sauce
1 tablespoon sugar
⅔ cup vegetable broth
1 teaspoon cornstarch mixed with 1 teaspoon water until smooth

Heat the oil in a large deep pan or preheated wok, and add the chicken, onion, garlic, ginger, bell pepper, and chili. Fry for about 5 minutes at high heat.

Add the soy sauce, wine vinegar, sherry, chili sauce, sugar, broth, and cornstarch to the pan and continue cooking over high heat until the liquid has thickened and the chicken is cooked through, about 6–8 minutes. Serve with noodles.

Serves 4

CHICKEN & BASIL CHILI

4 chicken quarters
3 tablespoons olive oil
1 red chili, seeded and finely chopped
1 tablespoon fresh cilantro root and stem, finely chopped
2 garlic cloves, minced
2 green chilies, seeded and finely chopped
2 tablespoons Thai fish sauce
1 tablespoon oyster sauce (optional)
small bunch fresh basil, torn into small pieces

Cut the chicken into smaller pieces using a large sharp knife or a meat cleaver.

Heat the oil in a preheated wok and fry the chicken until golden and almost cooked through. Remove from the wok. Add the red chili, cilantro, and garlic, and fry for a few minutes. Return the chicken to the wok and add the green chilies, fish sauce, and oyster sauce if using.

Cook over medium heat for 5–10 minutes or until chicken is completely cooked. Stir in the basil leaves and serve.

Serves 4

CHICKEN GREEN CHILI

SAUCE:
1 teaspoon light soy sauce
1 teaspoon dark soy sauce
salt, to taste
2 teaspoons cornstarch
1 teaspoon sesame oil
1 teaspoon malt vinegar
1¼ cups chicken broth
SEASONING:
salt and freshly ground black pepper, to taste
2 tablespoons dark soy sauce
1 tablespoon light soy sauce
1 teaspoon cornstarch
2 teaspoons rice wine or dry sherry
1 lb boned chicken, cut into bite-size pieces
3 tablespoons olive oil

3 scallions, chopped
1-inch piece fresh ginger, peeled and sliced
2 garlic cloves, sliced
1 green bell pepper, chopped
1–2 green chilies, sliced lengthwise and seeded

Mix the sauce ingredients together and set aside. Mix the seasoning ingredients together and add the chicken. Marinate for 10 minutes. Drain the chicken and discard the liquid. Heat 1 tablespoon of the oil and stir-fry the scallions, ginger, and garlic for 2 minutes. Remove to a dish.

Add the remaining oil and stir-fry the chicken for 3 minutes. Add the green bell pepper and chilies and stir-fry for 2 minutes. Add the onion mixture and the well-blended sauce ingredients and cook for 3–4 minutes, until the sauce thickens. Serve immediately.

Serves 4

CHILIES & STEWS

VENISON CHILI

1 1/3 cups dried black beans, soaked overnight
2/3 cup dried navy or cannellini beans, soaked overnight
2 teaspoons cumin seeds
2 teaspoons coriander seeds
2 teaspoons dried oregano
3 lb boneless venison, cubed
2 tablespoons olive oil
scant 2 1/2–3 cups meat broth
2 onions, chopped
3 garlic cloves, finely chopped
2 red bell peppers, cored, seeded, and cut into 3/4-inch squares
2–3 teaspoons chili powder, or to taste
2 (14-oz) cans chopped tomatoes
3 tablespoons tomato paste
1 teaspoon sugar

1 teaspoon salt
6 tablespoons chopped fresh cilantro

Drain the beans, place in separate pans, and cover with fresh water. Boil for 15 minutes, then simmer briskly until just tender. Drain; set aside. Dry-fry the seeds over medium heat until fragrant. Add the oregano and fry for a few seconds more. Lightly crush in a mortar and pestle. Heat the oil in a skillet (reserving 1 teaspoon) and fry the venison over medium-high heat for 15 minutes. Sprinkle with half the spices.

Fry for a few minutes more and transfer to a Dutch oven. Add the reserved oil and 4 tablespoons of the broth to the skillet. Wet-fry the onions, garlic, bell pepper, chili powder, and remaining spices over medium heat for 5 minutes. Add the onion mixture to the meat together with the tomatoes, tomato paste, sugar, salt, beans, and about generous 1 3/4 cups of the broth. Bring to the boil, cover and simmer for 45 minutes. Stir in the cilantro and simmer for another 5 minutes.

Serves 6

SZECHUAN CHILI

12 oz chicken breast meat, cooked
1 teaspoon salt
1 egg white
5 tablespoons oil
1½ tablespoons cornstarch
2 slices fresh ginger, peeled
2 small dried chilies
2 green or red bell peppers
1 fresh chili
2 tablespoons soy sauce
2 tablespoons wine vinegar

Cut the chicken into bite-size pieces. Mix the salt, egg white, 1 tablespoon of the oil, and cornstarch and rub evenly over the chicken pieces to form a thin coating. Chop the ginger and dried chilies. Cut the bell peppers into bite-size pieces.

Heat the remaining oil in a preheated wok. Add the ginger and chilies, and stir-fry for 1 minute. Add the chicken pieces, separating them while stirring. Add the bell peppers, soy sauce, and vinegar, and fry for 2 minutes. Serve immediately.

Serves 3–4

CHICKEN & RICE STEW

1 (2 1/4-lb) chicken
generous 6 1/3 cups water
10 oz frozen peas
2 large carrots (about 7 oz)
1 fresh tarragon sprig
1 fresh thyme sprig
1 fresh parsley sprig
1 celery leaves sprig
1 medium leek, white part only (about 4 oz)
2 shallots
salt, to taste
1 cup long-grain rice
1/4 teaspoon cayenne pepper
2 tablespoons finely chopped fresh parsley

Rinse the chicken and place in a pan. Add the water and bring to a boil. Reduce the heat and let simmer for 30 minutes. Skim frequently during this time. Peel and dice the carrots. Wash the tarragon, thyme, parsley, and celery sprigs, and tie them together. Trim and wash the leeks, and cut into rings. Peel and quarter the shallots. Add the bunch of herbs, leeks, and shallots to the pan, and season with salt. Cover and cook for another 30 minutes.

Wash the rice under cold running water. Remove the chicken from the stock and set aside. Remove the herbs and discard. Add the peas, carrots, and rice to the stock, cover and cook over low heat for 20 minutes. Skin the chicken and cut the meat from the bones. Dice the meat and add to the rice. Season with the cayenne and serve sprinkled with the chopped parsley.

Serves 4

CHICKEN GUMBO

½ cup vegetable oil
1 (3-lb) chicken, cut into 6–8 pieces
generous ¾ cup all-purpose flour
1–2 fresh green chilies, finely sliced
1 large onion, finely chopped
1 large green bell pepper, coarsely chopped
3 celery stalks, finely chopped
2 garlic cloves, minced
8 oz garlic sausage, diced
4 cups chicken broth
1 bay leaf
dash of Tabasco sauce
salt and pepper, to taste
5 oz fresh okra

Heat the oil in a large skillet and brown the chicken on both sides, 3–4 pieces at a time. Transfer the chicken to a plate and set aside. Reduce the heat under the skillet and add the flour. Cook over very low heat for 30 minutes, stirring constantly until the flour turns a rich, dark brown. Take the pan off the heat occasionally, so that the flour does not burn. Add the chilies, onion, green bell pepper, celery, garlic, and sausage to the skillet and cook for about 5 minutes over very low heat, stirring continuously.

Pour on the broth and stir well. Add the bay leaf, a dash of Tabasco sauce, and salt and pepper. Return the chicken to the skillet, cover, and cook for about 30 minutes or until the chicken is tender. Trim the okra and cut each into 2–3 pieces. If the okra are small, leave them whole. Add to the chicken and cook for another 10–15 minutes. Remove the bay leaf and serve.

Serves 4–6

CHILIES & STEWS

CHICKEN STEW WITH ZUCCHINI

3 half-chickens, prepared for grilling
2 tablespoons butter
1 medium onion, finely chopped
1 garlic clove
3 zucchini
3/4 cup easy-cook rice
4 cups chicken broth
salt and freshly ground white pepper, to taste
juice of 1/2 lemon
freshly grated nutmeg
1 bunch fresh basil

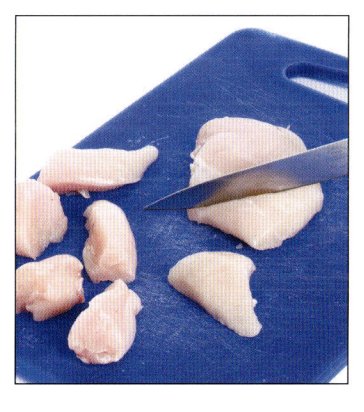

Skin and bone the chicken, and cut into small pieces. Melt the butter in a large pan and sauté the onion until translucent.

Press the garlic through a garlic press onto the onion. Rinse the zucchini, cut off the stem, and slice thinly on a vegetable slicer. Add to the other vegetables and stew briefly.

Mix in the chicken. Scatter the rice over the vegetables, stir in, and pour the chicken broth over it. Bring to a boil, and let simmer for 20–25 minutes. Season with salt, pepper, lemon juice, and nutmeg. Strip the basil leaves off their stems, and sprinkle them over the dish just before serving.

Serves 4

COUNTRY CHICKEN STEW

3 lb chicken portions
6 tablespoons all-purpose flour
3 tablespoons butter or margarine
8 oz pancetta, cut into ¼-inch dice
3 medium onions, finely chopped
7 cups water
3 (14-oz) cans chopped tomatoes
3 tablespoons tomato paste
4½ oz green beans, trimmed and halved
¾ cup frozen corn kernels
2 large red bell peppers, cut into small dice
3 medium potatoes, peeled and cut into ½-inch cubes
1–2 teaspoons cayenne pepper or Tabasco sauce, to taste
2 teaspoons Worcestershire sauce

1¼ cups red wine
salt and pepper, to taste

Shake the pieces of chicken in flour in a plastic bag to coat. In a large skillet, melt the butter. Add the chicken and brown over medium-high heat for about 10–12 minutes. Remove the chicken and set it aside. In the same skillet, fry the pancetta until the fat is rendered and the dice are crisp. Add the onions and cook over medium heat for about 10 minutes, until softened.

Pour the water into a large stockpot or pan and spoon in the onions, pork, and any meat juices from the pan. Add the tomatoes, tomato paste, and chicken. Bring to a boil, reduce the heat, and simmer for about 1–1½ hours. Add the beans, corn, bell peppers, and potatoes, cayenne pepper, Worcestershire sauce, and red wine. Season with salt and pepper. Cook for 30 minutes or until the chicken is tender.

Serves 6–8

POLLO CON PEPPERONI

4–5 fleshy green and red bell peppers
2 tablespoons butter
3 tablespoons olive oil
1 large onion, sliced
1 (2½-lb) chicken, cut into pieces
salt and freshly ground black pepper, to taste
⅔ cup dry white wine
3½ cups freshly chopped tomato pulp, or strained canned tomatoes
1 cup chicken broth
large handful of chopped fresh basil or parsley

Roast the bell peppers over a gas flame, or under the broiler until skin blisters. Rub the skins off with a paper towel.

Remove the seeds, and cut the bell peppers into 1-inch wide strips. Sauté the onion in the butter and oil until softened. Cut the chicken into serving pieces. Add the chicken pieces, and brown on both sides, Season with salt and pepper, and, when the chicken has browned, add the wine. Simmer until the wine has evaporated. Add the bell peppers, tomatoes, and another pinch of salt and pepper, then the broth.

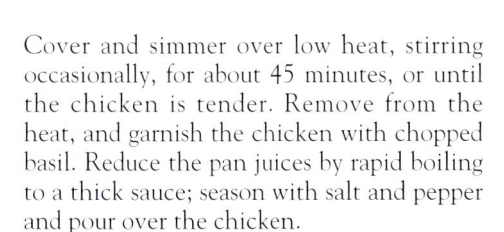

Cover and simmer over low heat, stirring occasionally, for about 45 minutes, or until the chicken is tender. Remove from the heat, and garnish the chicken with chopped basil. Reduce the pan juices by rapid boiling to a thick sauce; season with salt and pepper and pour over the chicken.

Serves 4

TOMATO CHICKEN

1 onion, peeled and chopped
3 tablespoons olive oil
1-inch piece cinnamon stick
1 bay leaf
6 cloves
seeds of 6 small cardamoms, ground
1-inch piece fresh ginger, peeled and grated
4 garlic cloves, minced
1 (3-lb) roasting chicken, cut into 8–10 pieces
1 teaspoon chili powder
1 teaspoon ground cumin
1 teaspoon ground coriander
1 (14-oz) can chopped tomatoes
1 teaspoon salt
2 fresh cilantro sprigs, leaves chopped
2 green chilies, halved and seeded

In a large pan, fry the onion in the oil, until it has softened. Add the cinnamon, bay leaf, cloves, cardamom seeds, ginger, and garlic. Fry for 1 minute. Add the chicken pieces to the pan. Sprinkle the chili powder, ground cumin, and coriander over the chicken in the pan. Fry for another 2 minutes, stirring continuously, to ensure the spices do not burn.

Stir in the remaining ingredients, mixing well to blend the spices evenly. Cover the pan and let simmer for 40–45 minutes or until chicken is tender.

Serves 4–6

RAGOUT OF TURKEY

1¾ lb turkey meat
3 tablespoons soybean oil
salt and freshly ground black pepper, to taste
1 onion, minced
2½ cups fresh mushrooms
2 teaspoons turmeric
½ teaspoon ground coriander
½ teaspoon ground cumin
1 (28-oz) can tomatoes
1 cup bean sprouts
1 bunch fresh basil

Cut the turkey meat into cubes about ⅔ inch across. Heat the oil in a wide pan and sear the cubes of meat, a few at a time.

Add salt and pepper, then the minced onion. Prepare the mushrooms, wipe, and halve or quarter depending on their size. Mix in with the turkey meat, then add the turmeric, coriander, and cumin. Chop the tomatoes, and stir them, and their juice, into the pan and bring to a boil. Cover, and let simmer for 15 minutes.

Rinse the bean sprouts. Mix in with the other ingredients. Cook the ragout for another 10 minutes. Meanwhile, rinse the basil, strip the leaves off the stalks, and fold them in just before serving. Serve with long-grain rice and salad.

Serves 4

THE BOOK OF

TURKEY STEW

1 lb 2 oz turkey breast
1 onion
8 oz mushrooms
1 tablespoon lemon juice
2 tablespoons sunflower oil
1 tablespoon butter
1 teaspoon cornstarch
1 teaspoon mild paprika
½ cup crème fraîche or sour cream
½ cup dry white wine
salt and freshly ground black pepper, to taste

Wash the turkey breast and pat dry. Cut into thin slices. Peel and finely chop the onion.

Thinly slice the mushrooms, and sprinkle with lemon juice. Heat the oil in a large pan, and stir-fry the turkey until brown on all sides. Remove from the pan with a slotted spoon and set aside. Add the butter to the pan and melt. Fry the onion until transparent. Add the mushrooms, cover, and cook over low heat for 10 minutes.

Mix together the cornstarch, paprika, and crème fraîche. Return the turkey to the pan, and stir in the crème fraîche mixture. Add the wine, and cook over low heat for a few minutes. Season with salt and pepper.

Serves 4

GAME STEW

8 oz grapes, white, red, or mixed
8 shallots
1½ lb game (venison or wild rabbit) off the bone
2 tablespoons clarified butter
salt and freshly ground black pepper, to taste
1 tablespoon Cognac or brandy
2 tablespoons dry white wine
½ cup light cream
1 teaspoon butter
1 teaspoon chopped fresh marjoram (optional)

Pull the grapes off their stalks, rinse, halve, and remove the seeds. Peel and chop the shallots. Cut the meat into ½-inch thick slices.

Heat 1 tablespoon of the clarified butter in a large skillet. Add the meat and brown quickly. Lift out of the pan and keep warm. Season lightly with salt and pepper. Pour the brandy into the skillet to release the juices and pour into a container. Put the rest of the clarified butter into the skillet, add the shallots, and sauté until soft but not brown. Add the white wine, bring to a boil, and reduce for 1–2 minutes. Add the cream and reduce until the sauce has a creamy consistency.

Return the meat to the sauce and adjust the seasoning with salt and pepper. Do not allow to boil, but keep warm over low heat. Heat the butter in another pan. Add the grapes and toss until heated through. Mix the fruit in with the meat, and serve sprinkled with marjoram.

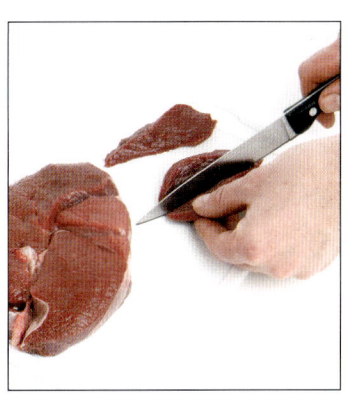

Serves 4

BLACK FOREST STEW

MARINADE:
1 cup chopped onions
1/2 cup chopped carrot
1/2 cup chopped celery
1 garlic clove, minced
2 whole cloves
1/4 teaspoon dried rosemary
1/4 teaspoon dried thyme
1 bay leaf
6 cranberries
5 peppercorns
1 tablespoon chopped fresh parsley
1/2 teaspoon salt
3 cups dry red wine
1/4 cup red wine vinegar
1/2 cup vegetable oil

STEW:
3 lb venison stewing meat
1/2 teaspoon marjoram
1/4 cup butter or margarine
1 cup chopped onions
1/4 cup all-purpose flour
1 cup beef broth
1/4 teaspoon pepper
1 cup sour cream

Place marinade ingredients into a 2-quart saucepan. Bring marinade to a boil. Reduce heat and simmer 10 minutes. Cool. Place venison and marjoram in a Dutch oven. Pour cooled marinade over meat.

Cover and refrigerate for 24 hours. Drain meat, reserving marinade. Pat meat dry. In a large pan melt the butter. When hot, add the meat and brown. Remove meat and brown 1 cup onions. Stir in flour, mix until well-blended. Add broth and 2 cups reserved marinade. Add pepper. Bring stew to a boil, stirring until slightly thickened. Add meat, cover, and let simmer about 1 hour, until meat is tender. Skim off fat. Add sour cream and heat through.

Serves 8

RUTABAGA STEW WITH DUCK

1 rutabaga (around 2¼ lb)
1 onion
5 tablespoons olive oil
4 cups chicken broth (preferably homemade)
4 duck breasts
salt and freshly ground white pepper, to taste
½ bunch fresh marjoram
1 bunch fresh parsley
2 small leeks

Rinse and peel the rutabaga. Peel and halve the onion and cut both into small dice.

Heat 3 tablespoons of the oil in a heavy-bottom pan and lightly sauté the onion and rutabaga over medium heat. Pour the broth over them and bring to a boil. Season the duck breasts with salt and pepper. Heat the rest of the oil in a skillet and sear the breasts over high heat for 2 minutes on each side. Add to the onion mixture and let simmer for about 10 minutes over medium heat.

Chop the marjoram and parsley finely. Rinse the leeks, and shred finely. Lift the duck breasts out of the sauce, and keep warm. Add the herbs and leeks and let simmer for 3–4 minutes, until the leeks are tender. Slice the duck breasts. Ladle the stew into heated plates, and arrange the meat on top.

Serves 4

GULF COAST TACOS

6 ready-made corn tortillas
vegetable oil, for frying
GREEN CHILI SALSA:
1 tablespoon olive oil
3 tomatillos, husks removed, sliced
1 garlic clove
1 oz fresh cilantro leaves
2 green chilies
juice of 1 lime
1/2 cup sour cream
pinch of salt and sugar
FILLING INGREDIENTS:
8 oz large raw shrimp, shelled
8 oz fresh scallops, quartered if large
1 teaspoon coriander seeds, crushed
1 shallot, finely chopped

salt and pepper, to taste
1/3 cup white wine
1 small jicama, peeled and cut into thin strips
fresh cilantro sprigs and lime, to serve

Heat the salsa oil in a small skillet. Sauté the tomatillos for 3 minutes to soften. Place in a food processor with garlic, cilantro, chilies, and lime juice. Puree until smooth. Fold in the sour cream, salt, and pepper and chill. Heat the tortillas (see page 12). Keep warm, standing on open ends to prevent them closing.

Place the shrimp, scallops, coriander seeds, shallot, salt, and pepper in a sauté pan with enough wine and water to barely cover. Cook for 8 minutes, stirring occasionally, until shrimp turn pink and scallops are opaque. Fill tacos with jicama. Arrange seafood on top of the jicama. Top with salsa and cilantro sprigs. Serve with lime wedges.

Serves 6

CRAB QUESADILLAS

2 (7-oz) cans white crabmeat, drained
1 green chili, finely chopped
salt and pepper, to taste
4 large flour tortillas
2 tablespoons chopped fresh cilantro
3 scallions, finely chopped
2 tomatoes, peeled and chopped
1 cup grated cheddar or Jack cheese

Preheat the broiler to medium. Put the crabmeat into a bowl and add the green chili. Season with salt and pepper.

To assemble, place 1 flour tortilla on a baking sheet or broiler pan and spread with half the crab mixture. Sprinkle with half the cilantro, half the scallions, half the tomatoes, and half the cheese. Top with a second tortilla and press down gently.

Place under the broiler until golden and crisp. Carefully turn the quesadilla over (the easiest way is to put a second baking sheet on top and invert together) and toast the second side. The cheese should be melted. Remove from the heat and cut into wedges to serve. Repeat with the remaining ingredients. To serve, cut into wedges.

Serves 4–6

MUSSELS CHILI

2 lb live mussels
1¼ cups water
1 lemon grass stalk, chopped
1-inch piece fresh ginger, peeled and sliced
4 dried kaffir lime leaves
CHILI SAUCE:
1–2 large red chilies, seeded and chopped
1 tablespoon chopped fresh cilantro root and stem
2 garlic cloves, minced
2 tablespoons olive oil
2 tablespoons Thai fish sauce
1 tablespoon sugar
1 tablespoon fresh basil leaves, chopped
2 teaspoons cornstarch mixed with a little water

Scrub the mussels and remove the beards, discarding any mussels with broken shells or those that do not close when tapped. Bring the water to a boil and add the lemon grass, ginger, and lime leaves. Add the mussels, cover, and boil for 5–6 minutes or until the mussels open. Drain, reserving 3 cups of the cooking liquid. Discard any mussels that have not opened. While the mussels are cooking, start to prepare the sauce. Pound the chilies, cilantro, and garlic together in a mortar and pestle.

Heat the oil in a preheated wok and fry the chili mixture for a few minutes, then stir in the fish sauce, sugar, and basil. Add the reserved cooking liquid from the mussels and the cornstarch mixture. Cook until slightly thickened. Serve the mussels with the sauce poured over them.

Serves 4

SHRIMP VERACRUZ

1 tablespoon olive oil
1 onion, chopped
1 large green bell pepper, cut into 1½-inch strips
2–3 green chilies, seeded and chopped
double quantity Taco Sauce recipe (see page 16)
2 tomatoes, peeled and coarsely chopped
12 pimento-stuffed olives, halved
2 teaspoons capers
¼ teaspoon ground cumin
salt, to taste
1 lb raw shrimp, shelled
juice of 1 lime

Heat the oil in a large skillet and add the onion and green bell pepper. Cook until soft but not colored. Add chilies, taco sauce, tomatoes, olives, capers, cumin, and salt. Bring to a boil and then reduce the heat and simmer for 5 minutes.

Remove the black veins, if present, from the rounded side of the shrimp with a wooden toothpick. Add the shrimp to the sauce and cook until they curl up and turn pink and opaque. Add the lime juice to taste and serve.

Serves 6

SZECHUAN FISH CHILI

1 lb whitefish fillets, cut into 2-inch pieces
pinch of salt and pepper
1 egg
5 tablespoons all-purpose flour, plus extra for dredging
1/3 cup white wine
vegetable oil, for frying
2 oz cooked ham, cut into small dice
1-inch piece fresh ginger, peeled and finely diced
1 red or green chili, seeded and finely diced
6 water chestnuts, finely diced
4 scallions, finely chopped
3 tablespoons light soy sauce
1 teaspoon cider vinegar or rice wine vinegar
1/2 teaspoon ground Szechuan pepper (optional)
1 1/4 cups light broth

1 tablespoon cornstarch dissolved in 2 tablespoons water
2 teaspoons sugar

Season the fish with salt and pepper. Beat the egg and add flour and wine to make a batter. Dredge the fish lightly with flour and dip into the batter, mixing well. Heat a skillet and add enough oil to deep-fry the fish. When the oil is hot, fry a few pieces of fish at a time and drain until all the fish is cooked. Add 1 tablespoon of oil from the skillet to a preheated wok.

Add the ham, ginger, diced chili, water chestnuts, and scallions. Cook for 1 minute. Add the soy sauce, vinegar, and Szechuan pepper, if using. Cook for 1 minute. Remove the vegetables; set aside. Add the broth to the wok and bring to a boil. Add 1 spoonful of the hot broth to the cornstarch mixture. Add the mixture back to the broth and reboil, stirring, until thickened. Stir in the sugar. Return the fish and vegetables to the sauce. Heat through for 30 seconds and serve.

Serves 6

CHILIES & STEWS

FISH STEW

1 onion
2 tablespoons butter
2 large carrots (about 7 oz)
2 medium-sized leeks
5 celery stalks
½ teaspoon saffron powder
generous 1 cup dry white wine
3 cups fish broth
salt and freshly ground white pepper, to taste
juice of ½ lemon
1 lb 5 oz fish fillets
5½ oz raw shrimp

Peel and finely chop the onion. Melt the butter in a large pan, and gently fry the onion for 5 minutes. Peel and thinly slice the carrots. Add to the pan and gently fry for another 5 minutes. Trim and wash the leeks. Slice diagonally into pieces ½-inch across. Trim, wash, and thinly slice the celery. Coarsely chop the celery leaves. Add the celery and leeks to the pan, and fry for another 3 minutes. Sprinkle over the saffron, and cook, stirring constantly, for 1 minute. Stir in the white wine and broth, and season with salt and pepper.

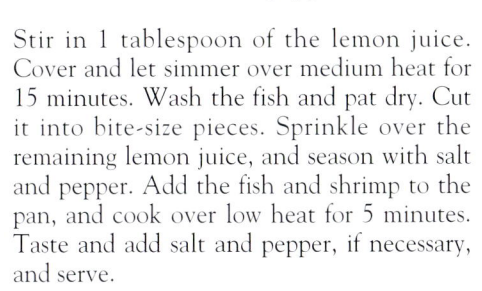

Stir in 1 tablespoon of the lemon juice. Cover and let simmer over medium heat for 15 minutes. Wash the fish and pat dry. Cut it into bite-size pieces. Sprinkle over the remaining lemon juice, and season with salt and pepper. Add the fish and shrimp to the pan, and cook over low heat for 5 minutes. Taste and add salt and pepper, if necessary, and serve.

Serves 4

THE BOOK OF

CREOLE COURT BOUILLON

1 lb bones from a white fish
1 bay leaf, 1 fresh thyme sprig, and 2 parsley stalks
2 onion slices
1 lemon slice
6 black peppercorns
1½ cups water
6 tablespoons vegetable oil
6 tablespoons all-purpose flour
1 large green bell pepper, seeded and finely chopped
1 onion, finely chopped
1 celery stalk, finely chopped
2 lb canned tomatoes
2 tablespoons tomato paste
1 teaspoon cayenne pepper
pinch of salt and allspice
6 tablespoons white wine
2 whole flounder, filleted and skinned 
2 tablespoons chopped fresh parsley

Place fish bones, herbs, onion, lemon slice, peppercorns, and water in a pan. Bring to a boil, then let simmer 20 minutes and strain. Heat the oil and add the flour. Cook slowly, stirring constantly, until golden brown. Add the green bell pepper, onion, and celery, and cook until the flour is a rich dark brown and the vegetables have softened. Strain on the broth and add the canned tomatoes, tomato paste, cayenne pepper, and salt.

Add the allspice. Bring to a boil and then let simmer until thick. Add the wine. Cut the fish fillets into 2-inch pieces and add to the tomato mixture. Cook slowly for about 20 minutes or until the fish is tender. Gently stir in the parsley, taking care that the fish does not break up. Taste and add salt and pepper, if necessary, and serve.

Serves 4

SEAFOOD STEW

24 fresh clams or 16 mussels in the shell
3 medium tomatoes, peeled, seeded, and chopped
½ green bell pepper, seeded and chopped
1 small onion, chopped
1 garlic clove, finely chopped
½ cup olive oil
1 large prepared squid
1 lb whitefish, filleted into 2-inch pieces
1 cup dry white wine
salt and pepper, to taste
4–6 slices French bread
2 tablespoons chopped fresh parsley

Scrub the clams or mussels to remove beards and barnacles.

Discard shellfish with broken shells or ones that do not close when tapped. Place the clams or mussels in a large pan, sprinkle over half of the vegetables and garlic and spoon over 4 tablespoons of the olive oil. Cut the squid into 1-inch squares and, using a knife, score a crisscross pattern on one side. Sprinkle the squid and the whitefish over the vegetables in the pan and top with the remaining vegetables. Pour over the white wine and season with salt and pepper. Bring to a boil over high heat and reduce to simmering.

Cover the pan and cook for about 20 minutes or until the clams open, the squid is tender, and the fish flakes easily. Discard any clams or mussels that do not open. Heat the remaining olive oil in a skillet and when hot, add the slices of bread, browning them well on both sides. Drain on paper towels. Place a slice of bread in the bottom of a soup bowl and ladle the fish mixture over the bread. Sprinkle with parsley and serve immediately.

Serves 4–6

BOATMAN'S STEW

6 tablespoons olive oil
2 large onions, sliced
1 red bell pepper, seeded and sliced
4 oz mushrooms, sliced
1 lb canned tomatoes
pinch of dried thyme
pinch of salt and pepper
1 1/2 cups water
2 lb whitefish fillets, skinned
1/2 cup white wine
2 tablespoons chopped fresh parsley
1 French bread baguette

Heat the oil in a large pan and add the onions. Cook until onions are beginning to become translucent. Add the bell pepper and cook until the vegetables are softened. Add the mushrooms and tomatoes and bring the mixture to a boil. Add thyme, salt, pepper, and water and let simmer for about 30 minutes.

Add the fish and wine and cook until the fish flakes easily, about 15 minutes. Stir in the parsley. To serve, either place toasted French bread on the side or place a piece of toasted French bread in the bottom of the soup bowl and spoon over the fish stew.

Serves 6

CHILIES & STEWS

PROVENCALE FISH STEW

- 1 medium onion, finely chopped
- 2 garlic cloves, minced
- 3 tablespoons olive oil
- 1½ tomatoes, peeled, seeded, and chopped
- 2 cups dry red wine
- 2 tablespoons tomato paste
- salt and pepper, to taste
- 8 oz fresh mussels in their shells, scrubbed and debearded
- 8 large shrimp
- 5 oz shelled medium shrimp
- 4 crab claws, shelled but with the claw tips left intact

In a large pan, fry the onion and garlic together gently in the olive oil, until they are soft but not brown. Add the tomatoes and fry until they begin to soften. Stir in the red wine and the tomato paste. Season with salt and pepper, then bring to a boil, cover, and let simmer for about 15 minutes.

Add the mussels, re-cover the pan, and let simmer for 5–8 minutes or until the mussel shells open. Discard any that remain closed. Stir in the remaining ingredients and cook, uncovered, for about 5–8 minutes or until the shellfish has thoroughly heated through.

Serves 4

THE BOOK OF

NEW ENGLAND BOUILLABASSE

BROTH:
1 lb fish bones, skin, and heads
7 cups water
1 small onion, thinly sliced
1 small carrot, thinly sliced
1 bay leaf
6 black peppercorns
¼ teaspoon ground mace
1 fresh thyme sprig or ½ teaspoon dried
2 lemon slices
BOUILLABAISSE:
½ cup butter or margarine
1 carrot, sliced
3 leeks, well washed and thinly sliced
1 garlic clove
pinch of saffron powder

⅓–½ cup dry white wine
8 oz canned tomatoes
1 lb cod fillets
1 lb live mussels, well scrubbed
1 lb fresh small clams, well scrubbed
8 new potatoes, scrubbed but not peeled
chopped fresh parsley
8 oz large raw shrimp, shelled and deveined

Place broth ingredients in a large pan and bring to a boil. Reduce heat and simmer for 20 minutes. Strain and reserve broth, discarding bones and vegetables. Melt the butter in a pan. Add the carrot, leeks, and garlic.

Cook for 5 minutes, until slightly softened. Add the saffron and wine and simmer for 5 minutes. Add the fish broth, bringing the mixture to a boil, add the remaining bouillabaisse ingredients except the shrimp. Bring the mixture to a boil and cook until the mussel and clam shells open and potatoes are tender. Turn off the heat and add the shrimp. Cover and let the shrimp cook in the residual heat. Divide the ingredients into bowls and serve.

Serves 4

CHILIES & STEWS

CREOLE VEGETABLE STEW

4 tablespoons olive oil or peanut oil
2 onions, diced
2–3 garlic cloves, thinly sliced
1 teaspoon coriander seeds
1 lb 2 oz young, fresh okra, trimmed and washed
3 beefsteak tomatoes, blanched, peeled, and diced
salt and freshly ground black pepper, to taste
juice of $\frac{1}{2}$ lemon
$1\frac{1}{8}$ cups long-grain rice
$\frac{1}{4}$ teaspoon saffron powder
1 clove
7 oz raw shrimp
2 tablespoons butter

Heat the oil, and fry the onions and garlic until transparent. Sprinkle over the coriander seeds and stir-fry for another 2–3 minutes. Add the okra and fry until it starts to soften. Stir in the tomatoes and season with salt and pepper. Cover the pan, reduce the heat, and braise the vegetables for 1 hour, until soft. Add the lemon juice.

Meanwhile, cook the rice for 20 minutes in plenty of lightly salted boiling water containing the saffron and clove. Drain. Shell the shrimp. Melt the butter, add the shrimp, and toss them briefly in the butter until colored. Combine the rice, okra, and shrimp in a large pan, cover with a lid, and let stand for 5 minutes to allow the flavors to mingle. Serve hot.

Serves 4

INDEX

Beef and Orange Chili 33
Beef and Pepper Stew 36
Beef Stew 41
Beef Stroganoff 38
Black and White Bean
   Chili 20
Black Bean Tacos 12
Black Forest Stew 82
Boatman's Stew 92

Chicken and Basil Chili 69
Chicken and Rice Stew 73
Chicken Green Chili 70
Chicken Chili with
   Tortillas 67
Chicken Gumbo 74
Chicken Stew with
   Zucchini 75
Chickpea and Eggplant
   Stew 22
Chili Bean Quesadillas 14
Chili Roja 35
Chili Verde 51
Chimichangas 66
Chinese Chili Chicken 68
Chorizo and Potato Chili 47
Country Chicken Stew 76
Crab Quesadillas 85
Creole Court Bouillon 90
Creole Vegetable Stew 95
Curried Pork Stew 57

Empanadas 32
Enchiladas 46
Exotic Rice Stew 26

Fish Stew 89
Flautas 65

Game Stew 81
Gulf Coast Tacos 84

Ham and Green Lentil
   Ragout 59
Hungarian Veal Goulash 40
Hunter's Stew 39

Lamb Ragout 64
Leek and Pork Stew 56
Lemon Pork Ragout 60

Mussels Chili 86

Nachos 31
New England Bouillabasse 94

Piedmont Beef Stew 45
Pollo Con Pepperoni 77
Pork and Bean Chili 54
Pork and Chocolate Chili 52
Pork and Lime Chili 49
Pork Rib Chili 50
Potato and Bean Stew 24
Provencale Fish Stew 93

Quick and Easy Chili 37

Ragout Bolognese 44
Ragout La Berghoff 42
Ragout of Turkey 79
Ragout of Young
   Vegetables 25
Ranch Chili 34
Ratatouille 23
Red Bean Chili 17
Roast Corn Chili Sauce 13
Rutabaga Stew with
   Duck 83

Sausage Chili 48
Seafood Stew 91
Sicilian Ratatouille 27
Shrimp Veracruz 87
Spiced Pork and Corn
   Chili 53
Squash and Black Bean
   Chili 18
Sweet Potato Burritos 15
Szechuan Chili 72
Szechuan Fish Chili 88

Tacos 28–9
Taco Sauce 16
Thai Pork Chili 55
Tofu Chili 19
Tomato and Chickpea
   Stew 61
Tomato Chicken 78
Tostadas 30
Turkey Stew 80
Tuscany Beef 43

Vegetarian Chili 21
Venison Chili 71

Welsh Stew 62–3